KU-473-941

Dear Jesus . . .
I'm So Human

Dear Jesus . . . I'm So Human

Rosanne E. Nelson

HODDER AND STOUGHTON
LONDON   SYDNEY   AUCKLAND   TORONTO

All biblical quotations are from the New American Standard Bible and the King James Version.

The author is grateful to World Books for the use of lines from Lord, Could You Make It a Little Better? by Robert A. Raines, copyright 1973 by Word, Incorporated, Waco, Texas.

Copyright © 1973 by Rosanne Eierdanz Nelson. First printed 1973. This edition 1974. ISBN 0 340 18516 3. All rights reserved. No part of this publication may be reproduced or transmitted in any form or by any means, electronic or mechanical, including photocopy, recording, or any information storage and retrieval system, without permission in writing from the publisher. This book is sold subject to the condition that it shall not, by way of trade or otherwise, be lent, re-sold, hired out or otherwise circulated without the publisher's prior consent in any form of binding or cover other than that in which this is published and without a similar condition including this condition being imposed on the subsequent purchaser. Printed in Great Britain for Hodder and Stoughton Limited, St. Paul's House, Warwick Lane, London EC4P 4AH by Richard Clay (The Chaucer Press), Ltd., Bungay, Suffolk.

To L.C.

Contents

About the writing of these letters...

The Christian life should be a more positive experience than we periodically encounter. And we ache for someone with whom to be honest and talk about what *is* rather than what *should be*.

One day, when I was especially in need of talking to someone, I tried to imagine what it would be like to speak to Jesus in person. What would I say to Him? How would I say it? If I could sit down and talk with Him, face to face, surely the conversation would be friendly, candid, and simple.

So, I decided to write these letters to Jesus with this thought in mind. He is my dearest friend, loved and longed for, who has gone away; and I'm bringing Him up to date about the everyday happenings in my life. In doing so I have found myself speaking to Him, not in flowery language, not covered up with theological jargon, not with 'Thees and Thous', but as I would speak to Him face to face in twentieth-century style. This, I believe, is the unaffected manner He seeks from those He calls His friends.

Christians are not exempt from wrestling with feelings of confusion, fear, doubt, hate, resentment. But frequently we hear that we should be 'above it all'. In examining the life of Christ and His teachings we discover all too often our attempts to meet the standard of His perfection are futile. Our efforts seem fruitless as we grapple with un-Christlike feelings and thoughts almost every day, so we browbeat ourselves.

We strive for the ideal, and our distressing failures day after day only add more fuel to the needless fire of self-condemnation that constantly reduces us to something less than men and women created in the image of God. We cultivate a stout negative, moan our deficiencies, and forget we are of high value to God. Why else would He send His only begotten Son to die for us to verify that worth?

Many times I have fingered each book on the shelf of the religious section of the bookstore, trying to find someone with whom to identify. There are many books to be found on how to be *more* loving, more faithful, more victorious, etc. Next to the Bible nothing has helped me more in my life than books by other Christians. We need the scholars, the philosophers, the theologians, the skilled writers to guide us and impart to us their learning. I thank God for them. There are so many times, however, when I search for a book wherein the author really dares to admit personal struggles and conflicts. I have found a few such writers, and there is a lot of comfort in discovering there are other Christians who desire to be faithful servants of Christ, only to be frustrated in the face of all their humanity.

We long to identify with other Christians in our problems, and we hunger for plain speaking; but we have an accomplished ability to walk around the truth about ourselves because we fear rejection. If we discover we can come to Jeus with the freedom to admit *all* of our thoughts and feelings, then perhaps we can learn to talk to each other, honestly, without sugarcoating our conversations with worn Christian clichés.

I sincerely pray the reading of these letters will help you as you walk with me through the dailiness of life— not with a mask in an attempt to conceal true feelings, not with a fear that Jesus would be shocked by my frankness, but just as I am—without pretence.

Throughout each letter I have tried to keep in mind my basic objective of simplicity and honesty. Sometimes in writing I would come to a point of asking myself, 'Now do I really want to be honest about this too?' I am so adept at dodging certain thoughts and feelings I have for fear of being rejected or not being thought a good Christian.

It would not make sense to write these letters without using the pronoun 'I'. Therefore, I do not apologize but hope as you read them you will see yourself as the 'I' and relate to your own walk in the Christian life.

The Apostle Paul said, in Colossians 3:2, 'Set your affection on things above, not on things on the earth.' None the less, we are still walking on the soil of this earth. Having our hearts in the heavenlies and our feet on the ground is certain to cause conflicts. I hope these letters are down to earth but up to God.

I will not always paint a rosy picture of victories and problems solved. The Christian life has not been like that for me. There will be pictures of defeat as well as triumph, sorrow as well as joy. But always there will be a reaching out to the Lord Jesus Christ, in whatever circumstances, whatever mood ... even when I don't *feel* like reaching.

R.E.N.

September 1972
Overland Park, Kansas

Acknowledgments

There are many people who have influenced my Christian life over the years. It is impossible to mention them all. For those of you I have left out, forgive me, and thank you—you know who you are.

The one person who encouraged me to write, more than anyone, is Dr. Grace Ketterman. Her friendship, counsel, fellowship, and love have been a godsend. She is one of the most unselfish women I have ever met. Even with her busy activities of being a wife, mother of three children, public speaker, and psychiatrist, she took the time to read my manuscript, offering corrections and suggestions. I thankfully accepted each one. She is a lovely example of a Christian who always goes the second mile, and I wish to publicly express my appreciation for her valued friendship and guidance.

Randolph J. Klassen is not only my pastor but a dear friend. His wisdom and teaching have had a tremendous impact upon my life. I thank God for him. The times we have spent sharing the Lord Jesus Christ, life's complexities and joys, and trying to see it all in the light of the Bible have left a deep impression. He has helped me so much with my human struggles in the Christian life. Frequently during the writing of this book I asked him for the benefit of his knowledge of the Scripture that helped in so many areas. I truly appreciate it. Any mistakes, however, are my own.

If it were not for Young Life, this book may never have been written. It was indirectly, through their ministry with teen-agers, that I became a Christian. Later, when I was on the Young Life staff at their headquarters in Colorado Springs, my life was touched deeply by many of their leaders. Most specifically, I cherish every loving memory of the founder and President of Young Life, Mr. Jim Rayburn, who is now with the Lord. His leadership, love, and friendship affected my life more than he ever knew.

Miss Bess Combs, who has celebrated her eighty-fifth birthday, and whom I lovingly refer to as 'my Bible teacher', will always have a warm spot in my heart. To sit at her feet and listen as she shared the Word of God with me was an invaluable experience. The blessings that her teaching gave me are second only to the rewards of her love and friendship through the years—and her prayers.

I would also like to thank Dr. Sherwood E. Wirt, editor of *Decision*, and all others with the Billy Graham Evangelistic Association who conducted the School of Christian Writing in Minneapolis. It was there that I received the encouragement and confidence to present my manuscript to an editor.

To so many dearly beloved friends I would like to say a word of thanks. To Mrs. Virginia Minter, whose listening ear is evidenced by the worn pathway between our houses, and who read my manuscript with enthusiasm and support. Mrs. Rosemary Stewart and Mrs. Janet Loper are valued friends and wonderful neighbours. Their hearts and doors have always been open. To Punk and Jean Pettigrew, who not only shared their love and fellowship, but their home when I lived with them in Colorado Springs. Though many years ago, it was a time and experience in my life I shall never forget. To Mrs. Sandie Yeomans, whose effervescent Christian life and fellowship has warmed my heart—thank you. And to Mrs. Connie Jean Carolan, whose friendship and trust I cherish.

And how can I thank my parents? From a small child they took me to church and 'brought me up in the way I should go'. They never held on too tightly, and let me be free to make my own discoveries as well as my own mistakes, and I love them for it.

To my son, Elliot, and my three stepchildren, Sally, Greta, and Clayton—thank you. They were so patient and undemanding during the time I spent writing this book. So much of what I have written is because of them, their love, and their presence in my life.

Finally, were it not for my husband, and his encouragement and confidence that this book would be published, I may never have had the persistence to finish it. So, to L.C., who has not only kept my feet warm at night, but my heart warm through the years, I lovingly and with much thanksgiving dedicate this book.

Rosanne E. Nelson

Dear Jesus . . .
I'm so Human

'.... licit sex usually runs a poor second to illicit; don't make any more comparisons than you can help. What you really need to practise is keeping promises...'

Robert Farrar Capon
Bed and Board

She's Having an Affair, Jesus

Dear Jesus,

This morning I got a phone call from a friend. She's ready to chuck the whole thing with her husband, and told me she was at the point where she really could leave him. It didn't do me one scrap of good to tell her she didn't mean it—because she does! She's having an affair, and she's a Christian. But aren't Christians human too, Jesus?

Honestly, every day I live I become more and more aware of the grief and heartache in this world—even among Christians. Frederick Buechner in *The Magnificent Defeat* spoke of '... the slow, unspoken pain of being human'. It just seems sometimes we get stuck in the glue we pour beneath our own feet.

You know, I can understand why my friend feels as she does—why a woman (or man) turns in that direction. I've felt that pull. You know that. It's not the answer; but temporarily, it certainly can look attractive. I guess this is a good time to thank you for being faithful and always there during those times of depression and desired flight I've experienced.

Yes, I can remember going through those weeks and months in our marriage when nothing anyone could say or do made me feel any better. I prayed. I was honest with you. I tried to find guidance from your Word. None of it seemed to do any good. Somebody

17

said the best way out of a difficulty is through it. Much to my doleful realization that is true sometimes. All marriages must go through it—surely. I've never talked to anyone who hasn't, at one time or another, gone through a sort of 'stage' in their marriage when it gets dull, unbearable, and anything but the thrilling, exciting, you're-the-only-one-in-the-world-for-me experience it started out to be.

The other day a friend said to me, 'Did you hear about so-and-so? They're getting a divorce. I'm shocked—just shocked!' Well, I'm not shocked any more when I hear it—Christian or no. I asked my pastor the other day what *one* problem stood out from all others in our congregation among those who came to him for counselling. He said it was marital problems. He went on to say that when there is a spiritual breakdown it usually reveals itself in marital difficulty and a lack of communication. Paul Tournier said in *To Understand Each Other*, 'Deep sharing is overwhelming, and very rare.' Why is that, Jesus?

All couples can recall those courting days when they would sit and talk for hours on end. In fact, L.C. asked me the other day, when Greta was out in the back yard talking to her boy-friend, 'What in the world do they talk about all that time?!' He forgot. We talked about feelings, beliefs, convictions, our childhoods, dreams, anxieties, loves, and hates. But what do you do when those getting-to-know-you days are all over and you *got to know him*? Well, I don't know, Jesus. I know what happened in our own marriage. But can't speak for the difficulties others have.

Looking back on it, I'm glad we went through that difficult period. It brought us closer than we'd ever been before. Oh, I didn't *feel* as I wanted to be able to feel again—as a girl with her first valentine on her pillow—all goose pimply and heart racing. And I missed that old, ecstatic feeling. I think most women do. We think about it anyway. So when we wake up some disenchanted morning and discover the goose pimples are gone—we look for them elsewhere. Or wish we could. And we feel strangled by the moral principles and Christian teachings that won't let us do it—comfortably. Or we ignore the principles and teachings and do it regardless. Then we suffer from guilt which we try to suppress or ignore. Or else we rationalize and justify our actions because we had all these drives and feelings roaring through us that we couldn't handle.

I know it must be a problem you're very concerned about, Jesus. You instituted marriage and told us we were to tie the knot and keep it tied. But you knew all along how difficult it would be for two people to live together in harmony and love until death parted them. I've thought about this a great, great deal, as you know. And in my pensiveness I came to some conclusions. It may not be the right answer or the most profound, but it has made a lot of sense to me. And it is this:

When we stick with our marriage through the thick and thin, determined to keep our vows, commitments, and love alive, we discover, gradually, over the years, that there is no such thing as growing UP—we just continue to *grow*. Your whole intention in setting up the situation of one man and one woman, together, throughout life, must have something to do with not being child*ish*, but retaining child-*likeness*.

Our little seven-year-old went down to spend a few days with his cousin. After he'd been there about three days he was ready to come home because he and his cousin were not getting on. Well, we made him stay a little longer, but eventually he could come back home and escape the unpleasant situation. It has occurred to me that everything else in life is pretty convertible. If we don't like the neighbours, we can move. If we don't like our jobs, we quit and find another one (if we're lucky). If we don't like the town we're living in, we can move to another. If we get tired of our car, we buy a different one. Last year's dress doesn't do for this year's party—so we get a new one. But this is not so easy in marriage. No trade-in on another model is possible without a lot of grief, heartache, sleepless nights, and consequences. We can't pick up our blocks and go elsewhere to play. Well, we *can*. But if we do, we are running away from the opportunity to mature into the lovely people you know we can be—*and will be some day*.

Marriage brings to the surface, as no other relationship does, all those traits that few others ever see—not the neighbour, not the boss, nor even a best friend. It may be a paradox, but there's something beautiful about being shown one's ugliness. It's as we see ourselves and each other realistically, and are willing to come to you—that you can do something about those unattractive traits and make us lovelier, little by little, day by day, and year after year.

Help my friend. I don't know what will happen. If I can help—I'm available. Maybe she will leave and marry this other man. I just wish that she and her husband could learn what L.C. and I were, by your grace, fortunate enough to learn. The goose pimples may be gone (although I noticed a few the other night), but those pimples are replaced with a smooth glow when two people develop a solid relationship of beauty, maturity, and lasting love—a love that is not dependent upon just feeling—but DOING and BEING.

Love,

Rosanne

What is True Spirituality, Jesus?

Dear Jesus,

Yesterday I ran about fifteen errands, took Clay to buy new school shoes, went to the grocery store, washed several loads of clothes, cleaned the garage floor, supervised the washing of fingerprints and bicycle tyre marks off the garage doors, picked up the usual litter, cooked breakfast, lunch, and supper, refereed a half-dozen arguments between a thirteen-year-old and a seven-year-old, tried to read the Bible a little, answered umpteen phone calls, and tried to scrub the pimples off my delayed adolescent face with a new facial cream I discovered.

About the time I was up to my elbows in a new box of Sugar Smacks digging for the prize in the package for Elliot—well, I just had to laugh. Good grief! Is this what it's all about? As a wife, mother, laundress, cook, and Christian (not necessarily in that order since I haven't figured out what the *order* should be), I just want a sense of accomplishment and of making a lasting contribution while I'm on earth. Instead I find myself at the kitchen sink trying to wash off the sticky Sugar Smacks that got stuck to the hairs on my arm, and shouting at our stupid dog (who's after some female in heat down the street) to go and lie down!

Before I know it the day is gone, and I ask myself: What did I do today that will count for eternity? How did I grow any more like you, Jesus? What did I contribute to your world today? Tell me about true spirituality, Jesus.

O Jesus, Jesus, Jesus! Why did you have to die on

that cross? Why couldn't you have stuck around for a few more centuries? I certainly need you. I wonder what it would be like if you were here now, and scheduled to speak at Kansas City's new Harry S. Truman Sports Complex in front of 80,000 people. Oh, I can just see you—dark wavy hair, thick sideburns, the latest in a double knit, polyester sports coat, wide tie, standing there—the stadium so quiet you could hear a pin drop. And you would say something to fill us with awe, such as, 'I'm God! I have come to seek and save the lost. I am the beginning and the end. I will be tried in the Jackson County Courthouse, found guilty, sentenced to death—and die. But I will not stay dead. I'm going to rise from the dead, and when you go to the cemetery to see my grave, there will be angels standing there and they will tell you I'm no longer there. I arose!'

And we would all sit there with bated breath, hanging on your every word, anxiously awaiting as you tell us how to solve our problems. Hmmm. I wonder. No, we probably wouldn't listen and believe any more than when it actually happened. There would be booing and shouts of derision.

And you would die. And what we would not realize was that it was by your choosing—not because you *had* to, but because you *wanted* to. Because you knew the only way you could redeem us was by showing us you could conquer death. Because you knew we didn't know how to live freely. We are bound by our own persistent failures. You knew we wouldn't even know how to die freely without the hideous bondage of fear. So, you would do it for us all—all over again, if you had to. (Oh, God forbid!) They couldn't see it clearly then, and we probably wouldn't see it clearly now—if you were here and died in 1973 and our modern media carried the news and spread it all over the world in a matter of minutes.

You know, Jesus, I don't like pictures or paintings of

the crucifixion. Not the ones I've seen. The cross, of course, has become symbolic. And that's O.K. But it's too pretty. Women wear the cross for earrings and necklaces, and we see the symbolic cross in beautiful stained glass windows. I'm not knocking it. But don't you think that because we have made it so symbolic in various ways it has lost its reality? The original cross wasn't beautiful stained glass. It wasn't gold. It wasn't silver. You didn't hang there in a sort of godly, silent serenity—did you, Jesus? Wasn't it bloody, sweating, painful, and dirty? Weren't you a man hanging there who was dying for a drink of water, or wine—something to quench your terrible thirst? Weren't you, for those hours, the most totally alone person who ever lived or ever will live? Suspended. Cut off. Then—you cried out and asked your own Father why He had forsaken you. I would have been anxious for death as a relief. Were you, Jesus? Oh, bring the reality of that scene back there on the hill down here where I live. Help me to comprehend what happened there in a mysterious mixture of horror and glory.

Then suddenly, we find you three days later walking down a country road, making conversation with some men who are talking about the terrible thing that happened to you. They are so involved in their anxiety they don't even recognize you. (I'm like that, too, sometimes. I get so involved in my problems I wouldn't recognize you if you stood right in front of me.) I see you smiling and inviting Thomas to touch your wounds. Your friends are elated, unbelievably happy to discover you actually did conquer death. And then, you ascend into heaven. A risen Lord. A risen Saviour. A risen God who was man—who returns to take His place above every name that is named.

Does that have something to do with true spirituality? The *fact* of it all and the *fact* that I believe it? The *fact* that I love you even though I can't see you at the Harry S. Truman Sports Complex or anywhere for

that matter? The *fact* that I KNOW YOU ARE THERE—
even though I can't prove it? The *fact* that I recognize
how weak, failing, and stupid I am at times? The *fact*
that I believe you see my heart that doesn't like my
sinning though I keep doing it—and you smile on my
divine discontent with my own life? Does all that and
the wonderful truth that you accept me with all my
imperfections have anything to do with true spirituality? I hope so.

Some glorious day I'll see your face as you explain it
to me. Meanwhile . . .

I love you,

Rosanne

'... that you may know ... what are the riches of the glory of *his* inheritance in the saints.'

Ephesians 1 : 18
New American Standard Bible

Thank You for Me

Dear Jesus,

There is something our seven-year-old always says in his prayers before he goes to bed at night. (Of course, you know what it is.) But it has really made me think. He says, 'Dear Jesus, thank you for Daddy 'n' Mummy 'n' Sally 'n' Greta 'n' Clay—and thank you for me.' You knew what you were talking about when you said a little child shall lead them. 'And thank you for me!' I've never said that to you before. I've thanked you for loving me, dying for me, and lots of other things—but I've never just thanked you for myself. So, thank you, Jesus. I can truly say that now with a sense of worth and value. Seventeen years ago I couldn't say it—or even two years ago. But now I know I do have great worth and value to you, as the one who created me, died for me, and lives for me.

As you know, I spent the early years of my Christian life around some rather rigid Christians. I love them, Jesus. And you know in my heart I don't judge them. They were just like the rest of us, I'm sure—struggling, striving, and doing their utmost to live the kind of lives they thought would please you, and teaching the fundamentals they felt important. I can well remember, however, lying flat on my back in the hospital, on the brink of a nervous breakdown, and a lady came to see me (a Christian lady). She stood beside my bed and said, 'Now, Rosanne, just straighten up. Christ must increase and you must decrease!' Bless her heart,

25

Jesus. She was trying, I'm sure, to say what she felt would be the most edifying words I could hear at the time. I'd only known you for about three years, and was such an eager beaver. All I could do was lie there in my bewildered, exhausted frame of mind and repeat over and over to myself, 'Christ must increase I must decrease.' Then I would quote other Scripture to myself. 'In my flesh dwells no good thing.' 'Our righteousnesses are as filthy rags.' 'The heart is deceitful and desperately wicked above all things.' All of those kinds of verses. Which, of course, are true. But that's only one side of the coin. It was years, you know, before I gradually began to see the other side.

Constantly, the emphasis was upon the negative and constantly I was told to 'be strong in the Lord'. Be strong! Be strong! Oh, if only I could! I wanted to; but how could I when I was so busy condemning myself and reassuring myself I was the lowliest worm and no-good sinner who just happened to be lucky enough to have a Saviour? O Jesus, let me be very careful and gentle with other Christians—especially young ones. Keep me from showing them only the negative.

Some years later, as the *truth* finally soaked in, I was sitting in my house one day, reading your book, and I suddenly exclaimed, 'Hallelujah, I'm not a worm!' I loved myself. You told us to love ourselves, didn't you, Jesus? Isn't that what you meant when you said, 'Love your neighbour *as* yourself'?

I think I started seeing that other side of the coin, little by little, in 1960 when I sat with my friend Bess Combs and studied the Bible with her. What a dear old saint and great teacher she is, Jesus. Thank you for her. It was going through the book of Ephesians with her that started me on the right track. That first chapter is loaded with verses for the other side of the coin. I guess if I had to pick my favourite book in the Bible this would have to be it. I can hardly catch my breath from one verse to the next.

'He chose us . . . according to his good pleasure . . .'
'. . . the riches of his grace . . .'
'. . . we have obtained an inheritance . . .'
'. . . you were sealed in him . . .'
'. . . the riches of the glory of his inheritance in the saints.'

Yes, Jesus, when I began to realize that *you* cherish *me* as your own and that you look forward to receiving *your* ultimate inheritance in me when I stand before you in heaven, fully redeemed by your work on the cross, it was the beginning of a new attitude. I could comprehend that *I* had obtained an inheritance in *you*, but to understand that you have a rich and glorious heritage in me is something else. It truly does take my breath away! The wonder of it all!

My pastor was pointing out to me a few months ago how you were often complimenting people when you were here on earth. The only ones you really let have it right between the eyes were the self-righteous Pharisees. But for the ones like me who already knew about their need and unworthiness—you loved them, helped them, encouraged them, complimented them, and pointed out their value and worth as your creatures. Thank you for your prayer in John 17: '. . . and all things that are Mine are Thine, and Thine are Mine; and I have been glorified in them . . . that they also may be in Us; that the world may continually believe that Thou didst send Me.'

'And this is eternal life, that they may know Thee, the only true God, and Jesus Christ whom Thou hast sent.'

Thank you for you. Thank you for eternal life. Thank you for me.

You are loved, Jesus,

Rosanne

You Weren't Glum, Were You, Jesus?

Dear Jesus,

I'm so excited I don't know where to begin! You know how I've been telling you for so long that I really want to know you—I mean *really*? Well, I thought you'd be happy to hear I'm finally making some progress. Or, to put it a better way, you're finally making some progress with me. You've had quite a job to do (not that it's completed) in getting rid of these cobwebs that have gathered in my brain. I've always been so stupidly solemn about Christianity, haven't I? All those preconceived notions I've had about you due to so much misguided piety are finally giving way to *truth*.

Remember once I told you I didn't like paintings of the cross because they're always too pretty? Well, I don't like most paintings of *you*, either. They usually make you look so sad and serious. Not that you weren't at times, but that's only a part of you. We have one picture of you in our home, however, and it depicts you as rugged, handsome, having strong features, a pleasant smile on your face, and looking like the kind of a man the big fisherman instantly wanted to follow. I picked it out because this is more what I think you really looked like rather than some glum, mild-mannered, dour, weak-looking man who never cracked a smile—let alone laughed. You weren't glum, were you, Jesus?

I've had my biased concept of you all neatly collected inside my brain and was so afraid to take the lid

28

off and let some light in for fear I might get mixed up with all those 'liberals' and have my ever-faithful fundamentalism attacked. After all, Christianity is a serious business, you know. (Though I have wrongly confused seriousness with rigidity and austerity.)

Now, thanks to those great authors, Matthew, Mark, and Luke, and some thoughtful study, I'm beginning to see what you were really like, i.e., your total personality, not just one part of it. I'd always thought of you as sort of serene, cool-headed, stable (to the point of being inflexible), quiet, unruffled, stern, endlessly patient, and cheerless. But the Gospel doesn't convey just that kind of picture. As I see it you were also jovial, capable of anger, a great storyteller (some of them quite funny), impatient at times, and your childlike zest for living is obvious in several portions of the Gospel.

As for being cool-headed—what about the day you got angry and threw the furniture down the stairs of the temple and asked those men how they expected to escape the damnation of hell?

As for being cheerless—what about that day at the wedding when they ran out of wine? You could have said, 'Oh well, we've all had enough partying anyway —let's go home.' But no! You turned the water into wine so the party could go on. Of course, I realize you did that partly to show your Deity—that you could perform miracles. But I can't believe you did it for that reason alone. People were having fun, and it was an occasion that called for celebration—and you enjoyed fun. Otherwise, why didn't you make an angel pop out of the wedding cake? That would have been an evidence of your ability to perform miracles. No—I think you were having a good time and you didn't want the party to break up so early and have everyone go home because they ran out of wine. I also think you felt sorry for the host and his embarrassment at not having enough wine for his guests.

And you were often eating and drinking with your disciples—as well as tax collectors and sinners—and you had a reputation for gaiety. (Your enemies even called you a drunkard.) I loved what you said to those Pharisees and experts on the Mosaic Law. Nobody could please them. You pointed out to them '... John the Baptist has come eating no bread and drinking no wine; and you say, "He has a demon!" The Son of Man has come eating and drinking; and you say, "Behold, a gluttonous man and a wine-drinker, a friend of tax gatherers and sinners!"'

As for being stern—what about all those delightful, witty stories you were always telling? I especially like the analogy about the scribes and Pharisees who cleaned the outside of the cup and dish and forgot to wash the inside. They strained out the gnat and swallowed a camel! That's funny! I can just see some pompous so-and-so sitting there making certain not to let that tiny gnat get into his drink and then downing two humps, four legs, a wet nose, and all that hair without even knowing it. (I've swallowed a few camels in my day, too.)

Or what about the time you were talking to your disciples about the fact that what goes into a man can't defile him? You said, 'Are you so uncomprehending? Do you not see that whatever goes into the man from outside cannot defile him; because it does not go into his heart, but into his stomach, and is eliminated?' That's a good one. Anybody should have enough sense to know that when something goes in one end it eventually comes out the other. That was a vivid and an amusing illustration.

As for being unruffled—what about the time you called those Pharisees hypocrites and said they were like '... whitewashed tombs ... full of dead men's bones and all uncleanness'?

You cried, you laughed (because I can't imagine anyone telling some of the funny stories you told with a sober face), you grieved, you enjoyed food and wine with your friends, you were impatient (the time when you thought you'd *never* get through to your disciples and you said, 'How long must I endure you?'!), you got tired and weary of mind; you could be extremely serious; and you could have fun. All of these things I'm discovering about you are dusting the cobwebs away. I wish someone would paint a picture of you illustrating one of those many scenes when you were with your friends—eating, drinking, laughing, and having a wonderful time of fellowship together.

Oh, don't ever let me be a glum Christian again. Let your delightful personality get through the sombre façade of this religious temple I hole up in sometimes. You must have a sense of humour to sit up there and watch the bumbling antics I pull sometimes. If there *isn't* any laughter in heaven ... well, may I have a rain check? (Just kidding, Jesus.)

I see blue skies, green grass, bright flowers, white clouds, moon, stars, sun, and rainbows. I feel gentle breezes, hear the bird's song, and a baby's laughter, and I see a dog's wagging tail. And I'm just beginning to see more clearly the exalted Maestro conducting the entire glorious symphony—you, dear Jesus!

> Keep teaching me,
> Rosanne

> 'O jealousy! Thou magnifier of trifles.'
>
> Schiller

I'd Never Liked That Woman

Dear Jesus,

We had communion at church last Sunday and it was more meaningful than usual. Elliot was excited too. He said, 'Oh boy, we get juice and crackers!' Well, you know and I know that it means more to him than that. He understands the meaning of communion as much as a seven-year-old can. But I wonder if it means much more than just juice and crackers to a lot of people—even Christians. Sometimes we just go through the motions, drink the juice (our church doesn't have real wine), eat the cracker, and think that it has something to do with your death on the cross. But the reality of the cross is way back there at a place called Golgotha and not here and now in the everyday happenings of life.

After communion our pastor encouraged us to show love. We turned around and said to the person behind us, beside us, 'God loves you.' So, I turned around, touched the hand of this man and his little girl behind me and said, 'God loves you.' The wonderful part about it was that I wasn't just saying some words. I really meant it. You really hit me with the beauty of your love for everyone.

Then I spotted this woman sitting two rows in front of me. I've never liked her. I don't really know why, but she's always rubbed me the wrong way. She seems so on top of it all, so secure, so sure of herself, so usable —pillar of the church and all that. As I sat there during the remainder of the service I kept thinking, 'God loves her.' As I said this over and over to myself I made a miraculous discovery. I loved her too! At that moment, I was able to look over whatever it was about her human qualities I had disliked for three or four years, and found, much to my delight, that I actually loved her—because you do, Jesus, and because your all-conquering love broke through the wall of my human pettiness.

Well, it may not sound like much. But to me it was, and I thank you for it. You were there last Sunday working inside my skin—weren't you? Frankly, I can't even remember what the sermon was about, although I'm sure it was good because they always are. But I remember where I was sitting, where she was sitting, and was aware that you loved through me.

After the service I went up to her (and I had to go out of my way to do it) and gave her a big hug and said, 'God loves you.' She smiled, hugged me, responded warmly, and I went away feeling as though a touch of heaven was inside me at that moment. I'm sure she wasn't aware of what had been going on in my heart that morning. I'm sure she had never known that I didn't like her. Thank you for reminding me in such a gentle, tender way that the people I don't like are people you died for and love deeply.

I didn't deliver a brilliant speech on your faithfulness and love, nor did I visit countless sick and lonely in the hospitals or homes for the elderly. And I didn't reach a dozen people last Sunday who had never heard of you. But I loved one woman. I genuinely, surprisingly loved her—and still do and am sure will henceforth. That's a lot—a whole lot. I understand better now what you meant when you talked about giving a cup of water to someone. It's seemingly insignificant. But it's so big in your eyes.

As I talk with other Christians, Jesus, I think many of them (including me) feel they should be doing big and great works for you. We reach for stars to put on our crown and ignore the midnight light burning in the window across the street when we know, or don't stop to think, that a person is there desperately needing love, comfort, or perhaps a listening ear. We dream of a great revival in our community or church but are too busy to sit down and give a thoughtful answer to the small child as he looks up and asks, 'Where did God come from?' We wish we could write a cheque for a thousand dollars to our favourite mission, yet we don't drive across town to take a pound of mince and a loaf of bread to a destitute family.

I'll never forget the day Martin Luther King was shot. I was shocked, sickened, and suddenly faced with the reality of this serious racial problem in our country. I wanted to buy radio or TV time and shout to the world how we must abolish our prejudices and love one another! Instead I got in the car and drove about eight blocks from our house where I knew a black family lived. There aren't many black families in our country. It's very affluent, as you know. Anyway, I walked up to the door with my little boy, rang the doorbell, and didn't even know what I was going to say. I introduced myself and she invited me in. I'm sure I must have muttered something about being sorry about what happened and that as a white person I somehow felt responsible. I'll never forget how kind and understanding she was. I don't know how she made much sense out of what I was trying to spit out, but she knew—she knew.

Thank you for Paul's beautiful admonition in Philippians 2:3-5. 'Do nothing from selfishness or empty conceit, but with humility of mind let each of you regard one another as more important than himself; do not merely look out for your own personal interests, but also for the interest of others. Have this attitude in yourselves which was also in Christ Jesus.'

Thank you for the words you left us. Some days they make their way into my heart and I see their truth as a reality. Other days, because of my own selfishness and wilfulness, they mean only a little more than nice, good thoughts. Just as some days my prayers seem to hit the ceiling and bounce back at me. Then other days, my attitude changes, and I know you heard after all, and you do and always will answer my prayers—according to your love and wisdom.

Oh, this is quite a life you have given us to live, Jesus—with its ups, downs, rounds, and abouts. Remember the other night when I was washing my pillow with tears? I'm not blowing my own trumpet because I know it was your spirit working with my spirit. Although I felt low, miserable, and confused, I was able to thank you; and I knew you were right in there with me and you would never, never leave me. Why is it that when I am able to muster up a genuine thank you in the midst of misery that my attitude changes and my grumbling turns to gratitude and praise?

Gratefully,

Rosanne

'... there's a yearning in me
a longing to let my sighs lengthen into songs
cascading through creation
ricochetting off the stars
echoing in human hearts and
resounding in my heart with a joyous Amen!'

Robert A. Raines
Lord, Could You make It a Little Better?

It's Good to Be Alive, Lord

Dear Jesus,

I'm glad I can say things right out to you and not have to worry about whether you think I'm silly. It's so good to be alive, Lord! There is so much feeling, yearning, dreaming, hoping, and loving boiling inside me. So many fantasies and images, and secret, deep-down thoughts I need to get out. Nothing bad—just so private I wouldn't know whom to say all these things to—if I knew how. I could try and tell L.C. But he's so much a part of me it's rather like talking to myself. And that won't do—talking to myself. I want to talk. I need to! But I want a response. Do you know what I mean, Lord? You'll respond—won't you? I won't hear any audible voice—or feel your strong arms around me assuring me that you do understand (not now, since you've gone away), but I know you do. I feel it in my insides—*you*—*there*—responding to me, Jesus. And though you already know, you still want to hear. You still want me to tell you all about it. What kind of Lord are you, Jesus?

Listen, Jesus. I'll try and pour it all out just now. It's hard to put feelings into words sometimes. But you gave me this womanly heart, and I'll reach inside of it now and share with you my intimacies. I'm not afraid to do so with you, Lord. You were intimate with me. What could be more personal than giving your life for me? The least I can do now is give you my thoughts . . . *all* of them.

Walt Whitman said, 'I contradict myself. I am large. I contain multitudes.' Henri Bergson said, 'The tools of the mind become burdens when the environment which made them necessary no longer exists.' The Apostle Paul said, 'I do not understand my own actions.' And I say, Lord, 'I do not understand my own thoughts.' But I don't apologize for them—because they feel good, Lord. They're not a burden to me—not when I can share them with you. Let me do that now. There's this beautiful image in my mind, Lord . . .

It's early summer. I'm with my beloved. We're sitting in a field of wild flowers high in the mountain meadows. I love it there! I want to take my shoes off and run barefoot through the flowers and shout—shout, 'Oh God—I'm alive! I live. I love. I'm a part of all this. It's a part of me. Let my soul mingle with all this beingness!' (Sound silly, Lord? That's me. That's what I dream about sometimes.) Hand in hand we would walk—talk—sing—live—play—run—rest. We'd marvel at the glorious things we are—sharing our emotions as one before you. Together we would watch a handsome herd of elk high above the timber line—mating, grazing, resting—storing up enough good life to see them through the long winter months ahead. Can we do that, too? Can we soak up enough blue skies, fresh air, waterfalls, wild flowers, grass, clouds, wind, and cool, star-bursting nights to see us through a winter of concrete, traffic, telephones, TV, appointments, and responsibilities? We'll try.

He'd chase me to a point overlooking an ocean of snow-capped peaks, and panting, we'd cast ourselves on the earth with hardly enough breath left for one long kiss. I'd thank him—he me—and both of us thanking you—for this garden of days and nights—the song of mountain silence pouring upon us as a sign from heaven that you bless this relationship and are happy for us in our love.

See what I mean, Jesus? How could I say to even my closest friend such things as that? Would anyone understand? Perhaps—since they probably have kept hidden, inside their own personal world, thoughts, images, and dreamy little visions. But still, Lord, people just don't go around talking to each other about it. I can only write it all down for you to see. If I walked up to someone and said, 'I love breezes, puppy dogs, dusty autumn roads, hugs, and hayrides—with wishes for star dust sprinkled on my head and moonbeams dancing on the lawn'—they'd think I'd taken leave of my senses! Wouldn't they?

But you don't, Jesus. With you, I can just sit down as I am now and tell you all about my fancies, notions and little scenes that pop into my mind while I'm going about the business of reality. Oh—and it feels so good to just let it out, Lord! Just to be able to tell you ... I want to run through the woods, looking at the sun's rays streaming from the treetops, feel the breeze in my hair, the moisture of dripping, wet leaves on my face, and I want to find a little spot to snuggle up in where my sounds will only be heard by you, Jesus. And I want to say all kinds of things out loud—just to free them from the bondage of my inhibitions. Maybe I'd just sing every song I could think of—one after another. Maybe I'd reminisce about my dog Prince (when we would sit on the garage roof together and find elephants in the clouds)—or my pony, Pat—or my cousin whom I loved and missed so as a child when he was away fighting in World War II—or talk of my first love.

What is it in me, Jesus, that loves all this? What is it in me that makes me stop, dead still in my tracks, marvelling at a little squirrel with an acorn between his feet? Isn't that you in me, Jesus—beholding your masterpiece? Isn't it something you put within me that wants to gather in, adore, and clap my hands, giving expression to the glory of your creation?

Thank you, Jesus, that all these fantasies can be liberated at your eager, listening ear. Thank you for not laughing at me—making me feel like a foolish, romantic female in the Land of Nod. Thank you for rejoicing with me in all of nature. Thank you for appreciating my desire to be sensitive to all of life's sounds and movements. Thank you for understanding how much I appreciate my womanhood—enjoying this feminine heart you've given me. A woman's heart—which melts at the beautiful softness of a baby's bottom—or cries at the crescendo of a symphony. A woman's heart—so complex, so vulnerable, so idealistic, so illogical.

You made me with the capacity to *feel* something in the presence of a fire's glow and crackling wood. You made me with the intuitive instinct to know when all that is needed is a gentle stroke of my hand to impart hope, courage, and comfort to my loved ones. Thank you, Jesus. And you even made me with the deep need to be needed, loved, wanted, adored—and told I'm the most beautiful creature in the world (although I know I'm not).

Let me go on, Jesus. I don't want to stop yet. There are more images still—more dreams. I need to let go of them. Don't you want me to give relief to all these pent-up, womanly wishes?

I've always wanted to roll up my jeans, dig my toes in the sand, and wish that time would stand still for a split second (like a moving picture when you stop it) just as the waves hit hard against me—splashing in my hair and face. Or I've wanted to run, hand in hand, with the love of my life, down a busy city street, everything covered with snow, stick out my tongue to catch the flakes, and shout to all the people passing how glorious it is to be a part of God and creation. I wish I could, Jesus. A child could, perhaps. People would only remark, 'How sweet—how charming—how cute,' if a child did that. Why do we lose those childlike qualities, Lord? Why do we become so staid and inhibited? When you talked about our becoming as children, didn't you mean that you want us to be united to you, as our own children are to us, in a unique freedom to just be *ourselves* and 'be at home with you'? The other day Elliot asked me why we couldn't get in the car and go around the city and pick up all the homeless dogs and cats and bring them to our house to live. When he asked the question he didn't think about whether I would consider his notion 'silly'. He *felt* it. And I have feelings too, Lord, and when I come to you, as *your* child, I don't worry about whether you'll think *my* notions are silly.

I remember once when L.C. and I were leaving a cinema. There was a can on the sidewalk. I kicked it— he kicked it—and we walked for two blocks to our car, playing kick the can. Two adults—having fun like children, enjoying ourselves and our little game. I'll never forget that, Jesus. Or I remember the time L.C. and I decided one soft spring evening to get our sleeping bag and spend the night outside in the back yard under the stars. What precious memories—romantic moments. So, it isn't *all* just dreaming and wishing, is it, Jesus? There have been very real experiences— childlike, wholesome, wonderful.

I guess this is my realm of reverie—my wonderland of delights after all. It's not *just* inside my mind. Some of it comes to life during those moments of tossing aside all our adulthood and letting that muzzled child in us experience the wonder of just being.

It *is* wonderful—just to *be*, to *belong*, to *become* childlike before you.

Your child,

Rosanne

> 'Marriage is the most complicated of all human relationships. Few alliances can produce such extremes of emotion or can so quickly travel from professions of the utmost bliss to that cold, terminal legal write-off, mental cruelty.'
>
> Thomas A. Harris, M.D.
> *I'm Ok—You're Ok*

At Home: We Laugh, Cry, Scream, and Pray

Dear Jesus,

I wish you could come for supper tonight. I'd send out for some Kentucky Fried Chicken so I wouldn't have to mess with cooking and dishes and we could talk until dawn. I've got so much to tell you! And lots of questions.

It's been one heck of a year for me—for all my family —which includes my husband, four children, a dog, cat, two gerbils, numerous toads from time to time, and an occasional turtle. I put my foot down on snakes. I told our seven-year-old he could have me or the snake—one of us had to go. After a few seconds of pondering he chose in favour of me. I was holding my breath for a while. I guess you understand that feeling, don't you, Jesus?

To begin with, about a year ago my three stepchildren came to live with us. Now we have 'yours and ours'. Thank goodness we don't have 'mine'. I don't think I could stand it. Anyway, having been used to just one little boy then adding three more overnight has been quite an adjustment. Just think. One in primary school, one in junior school, one in high school, and one in college. I knew it wouldn't be easy. But I didn't know it would be this hard, either! When we found out they were coming I told L.C., 'Well, I'll either find out what the grace of God really is or you can come and visit me at the hospital.' I think I'm finding out what your grace is—but it's a slow process.

There's no need to go into all the details. It's been pretty much as you would expect. Good times and terrible times. We've laughed and we've cried, we've screamed and we've prayed. Sometimes we can sit down and actually talk out differences. Other times we make a miserable attempt at sophisticated, twentieth-century communication. Some days I wanted to get on a jet plane and (pardon my expression) let the whole damned thing go hang! But I couldn't figure out where to go. Other days I've been able, somehow, to read about you, your life, and all the 'how tos' you taught, and I've been reassured it's all worthwhile. I seem to hear you say, 'Just stick in there, girl. I never told you it would be easy.'

I've made some terrible mistakes. It's easy to justify them because of the big adjustment and all that. But somehow I keep thinking, 'You should have been able to do better.' You know me. I love to browbeat myself. It would be nice if I could learn once and for all times what you meant when you talked about abiding in you and bringing forth fruit. I am learning, Jesus. But do you think I'm learning as quickly as I should? If you're satisfied with my rate of maturing as a Christian, I suppose I should be too. I keep forgetting you're not in the great big hurry that we are down here.

Just last Sunday we had a terrible scene. Oh, how I hate those scenes. Fortunately, we don't have them often. It had been building up inside me for months, actually, and I finally let the fur fly. I was so angry at Sally I told her if she couldn't take the heat to get out of the kitchen. (She's our eighteen-year-old.) I really let her have it. I was far from being loving, and I should have been more adult about the whole thing—but I wasn't. Woe is me, as old Isaiah was always saying. But we learned from it and it turned out O.K. Last night Sally and I even chuckled about it, and I was actually able to swallow my pride long enough to spit out a few words about how nice she is and point out her good qualities. You know, Jesus, I couldn't do that if it weren't for you. I don't understand how you work it, but your presence is felt, and your love somehow gets into my heart and out to others. I not only learned a little more about accepting another's weaknesses and faults, but something more about forgiveness. It seems each time I am sincerely able to forgive someone I give just that much more of myself. Just as you give more of yourself every time you forgive me. Anyway, it's certainly hard sometimes to give in and say, 'I was wrong, I am sorry.' And I was sorry I blew up the way I did.

You know I have to be honest with *you*, Jesus. You know all about it anyway. Our marriage has gone through a terrible strain this past year. Not that we've ever considered splitting the sheets, but we've had some real sessions and burned the midnight oil many nights trying to work things out between us. It's not that I ever quit loving L.C., but he just didn't light my fire any more. It wasn't his fault. I'm not sure it was mine either. It was just something that was happening. I even daydreamed about having an affair with another man. And I'm sure L.C. thought at times how nice it would be to find some sweet young thing to make him forget his problems too (at least temporarily). But that's an escape, and I know of no instance where it has been successful.

I was able to share my feelings with a friend and she told me it would pass—that all marriages go through it. Well, it did pass, and it's better than ever. It's really wonderful to go to bed at night, roll over into his arms, and think, 'I've got me quite a man!' You don't get an opal without cutting and polishing and lots of hard work. When you're through, you really have something to behold!

43

In my single days and during the early years of my Christian life, I always thought that if two people got married and they were both Christians, everything would be just dandy. Not so. I know it, you know it, and I'm sure most all Christians know it. Yet it seems to be a subject that isn't openly discussed in church. And I'm not sure an open discussion would be the answer. But all Christians, everywhere, need to realize their marriage isn't the only one in Christendom that gets a little rough at times. Just being aware of that might keep one from pushing the panic button.

There have been so many books written on marriage and the home. I'm certainly not going to try and add to it all. But Jesus, if we could learn to run (and I do mean *run*) to you quickly and read again 1 Corinthians 13, just maybe, *maybe*, we would find there a grand summation of all the books ever written on the subject of love.

Love is patient, love is kind, and is not jealous; love does not brag and is not arrogant, does not act unbecomingly; it does not seek its own, is not provoked, does not take into account a wrong suffered, does not rejoice in unrighteousness, but rejoices with the truth; bears all things, believes all things, hopes all things, endures all things. Love never fails.

Perhaps that's trying to make it sound too simple. But I know from my own marriage and personal experience, every time there is a problem of any kind, it's because one or more of those qualities of love you set out in your Word is missing in my attitude.

Show us how to bring our attitudes to you honestly and realistically. Remind us to come running.

Love,
Rosanne

44

'If we had forgotten the name of our
God, or extended our hands to a strange God;
Would not God find this out?
For He knows the secrets of the heart.'

Psalms 44 : 20 and 21
New American Standard Bible

The God of Romance

Dear Jesus,

Show me today how to cultivate the fruits you have given me through the Holy Spirit. Please don't allow me to cultivate futile desires and wish thoughts that will have no value in eternity. This day let me know you, not just as Saviour—but as Lord of my life. You said, before you left, that the Holy Spirit would teach me and bring to remembrance all the things you taught. I do so want Him to teach me. I just haven't learned fully yet how to hand over the reins to Him. I keep trying to hold on to them myself and then I make a mess of things.

Some days I don't care what happens to me—I hate myself so. I just don't want to hurt others. Forgive me for hating myself. That must cause you deep concern, because I know I am 'accepted in the beloved'. Ephesians still takes my breath away as I read that *you* have an inheritance in *me*.

But my heart and hands and every emotion within is crying out today for other gods. Thank you for Psalms 44: 20 and 21. Let me paraphrase that in a personal way. 'If I have forgotten the name of my God, or stretched out my hands to a strange god; will you not search this out in me—for you know the secrets of my heart.' I'm emotional, Jesus—you know that. I'm so aroused—wanting to search and stretch out my hands

45

to the god of romance and make-believe. I want to run away to never-never land, but know not where to find it. Even if I could, it would never fulfil me. I know enough about you and what you taught to be assured of that, dear Jesus. So why do I still search for it, dream about it, and ache inside?

O Jesus, I don't want to desire anything that is not your good, acceptable, and perfect will. Then why did you make me with the capacity to want what is not of you? When you created me anew in yourself, why didn't you remove the conflict? I don't understand! You have called me to serve you, to be a living response to you, and have given me so much. I want to live for you who died for me. But I don't know the 'how to'. Not in every area. But I can rest in your promises and their blessed security. Thank you for your life in me which causes me to trust you for *who* you are even though I am sorely confused at times. I've been told by other Christians and have read that if a person is confused and worried, then he is not trusting. But I'm trying, Jesus, I'm trying. '...he which began this good work in you will perform it until the day of Jesus Christ.' There's my answer, isn't it, Jesus? You've only begun—only begun; and it will not be completed until the day I am with you for ever in eternity.

Don't let me be consumed by my emotions today, Jesus. Don't let me '...go out with haste, nor go by flight...' without remembering '...the Lord will go before you; and the God of Israel your reward'. Jesus, go before me today in each step, each action, each reaction, each consuming desire. Keep me walking with you.

I don't know what to do with my emotions, Lord—I can't handle them on my own. '...neither know I what to do but my eyes are upon you.' Keep me from acting upon desires born out of needs I don't understand—for this will bring my downfall, and the hurting of others whom you love and died for—and are alive for today.

You're teaching me, Jesus, little by little, through painful steps, that I cannot expect all my needs to be fulfilled in other people Nor can I fulfil all their needs. Thank you for not giving us the burden of that responsibility, but inviting us to '. . . cast your burdens upon the Lord'. Forgive me when I try to have all my needs fulfilled in my beloved husband. If that were possible then there would be no need of the Holy Spirit whom you gave me.

Touch my heart today with your gentle hand. Strike a match of your living light, and show me how to cope with all these mysterious yearnings buried in my soul. Remove the drive within forcing me to seek cool waters and tender grasses from other than your precious self. Lead me quietly and lovingly to keep in step with you when my feet would run to other pastures for pleasant grazing. Heal my wounds and mend my broken heart. Dry my tears with the cloth of your comfort. Fogive me for the passing minutes, hours, sometimes days, when I feel sure another could be sweeter to me. Pour forth the oils of sweet-smelling Jesus-love and let me know that none other may ever care for me nor want my love as you do. Thank you for your alluring call to come away and be your beloved. And let me not seek from another what only you can be to me. My beloved, my Jesus.

All my love,

Rosanne

'One of the highest functions of a wife is to console her husband for all the blows he receives in
life. Yet, in order to console, there is no need to
say very much. It is enough to listen, to understand, to love.'

Paul Tournier
To Understand Each Other

A Thorn or a Lily?

Dear Jesus,
   'As the lily among thorns, so is my love among the
daughters.' Thank you for thinking of me in that way,
Lord. Actually, I feel more like a thorn than a lily
much of the time. I guess I'll never be able to fully
comprehend just how much I do mean to you.
   Last night I was a real thorn—in my husband's flesh,
that is. Do you know what I did? Well, I really had the
blues yesterday. I always get down in the dumps when
I hit one of those cyclic lows we women all experience.
I know your grace is sufficient for that too and I try
not to use it as an excuse for my lousy disposition. I
also know I should plan ahead and do some practical
things, e.g., allow extra rest, medicines (but you know
I'm not a pill-taker), and mark it on my calendar so I'll
remember to warn my hubby about those days.
Frankly, there are times when I'm kind of like Rachel
—'. . . she refused to be comforted'.
   Anyway, when L.C. came home from work I was
really grouchy. I was in one of those go-away-and-leave-
me-alone moods. Poor man. He'd had a rough day at
the office and I offered him no peace and love at all . . .
let alone the possible anticipation of making love. I
felt it. But I couldn't see my way clear to forget my
own feelings and think about his. We didn't say two

48

sentences to each other last night, and I went to bed at nine-thirty. I remember his crawling into bed around eleven-thirty. I guess I wanted to reach over and touch him—offer him some kind of warmth. But selfishness kept me from it. I was too engrossed in how blue and miserable I felt. Forgive me. Tonight I'll ask *his* forgiveness too and try and make it up to him. When he walks through that front door tonight after work, I'll give him a big hug and kiss, and listen as he tells me about his problems at the office.

I do abhor those monthly moods. Yet I find myself their victim every month. How is it women have been bogged down with this hormone bit? Do you realize I spend one third of my life down in the dumps because of this cycle we women are subject to? Of course, I know you realize. I guess I can blame it all on Eve. But poor Eve. She certainly takes a lot of guff. I'd probably have done the same thing if I'd been in her shoes. A woman's curiosity is just too much at times. Be it an apple or a letter to my husband marked 'personal'. Somehow I find it terribly difficult to resist.

If I didn't know you so well, and know you have every hair on my head numbered, I couldn't talk to you about such things. But after all, you are my 'Problem Solver', and this is a very real problem. I know you won't do anything about the way I'm made. I suppose I just wanted to ask you to remind me, during those days, that it's not going to last for ever and relief will come. My neighbour and I have to laugh about it when we're chatting over a cup of coffee. She sits there fanning herself because of hot flushes and I drip tears in my coffee because of the monthly blues.

Anyway, it's good that I can reaffirm certain truths, certain facts, and not worry too much about the injustice of womanhood. So, right now, I reaffirm the fact that you are Jesus, the Lord, the Saviour. Mine. You ascended into heaven and you live now to make intercession for me. You remain the same—yesterday, to-

49

day, and always.

Yes, life gets terribly trying and confusing at times. I read all kinds of books about the Spirit-filled life, yieldingness, faith, trust, hope—the adventure of finding out what it really means when Paul said, '. . . know Him and the power of His resurrection.' I know these facts to indeed be truth. Some days, Lord—well, I only can know it in my head. Putting the truth into a living experience is something else. It scares me. I fear you will put me aside no longer able to be used, no longer an earthen vessel whereby you may extend your warmth and love to others. I know better. I know you're not that kind of Saviour. But some days I feel just burnt out. Empty. Wondering why I was ever born, yet knowing all the while what your reason is for my life. A walking paradox.

Thank you for hope which persists in face of all adversity. Thank you for the knowledge of your love that prevails in the face of all my own lovelessness. And thank you that some days you hit me with the truth that to you I really am lovely—even on 'those days'!

Hoping to be more of a lily,

Rosanne

'Like a crane or a swallow, so did I chatter: I did
mourn as a dove: mine eyes fail with looking upward: O Lord, I am oppressed; undertake for
me.'

Isaiah 38 : 14
King James Version

I'm Sick of My Failures

Dear Jesus,

I'm so tired of Christian clichés. We throw them
back and forth at each other unthinkingly. Trust in
God, commit it to the Lord, pray about it—are all
good admonitions. It's so easy to give this kind of ad-
vice to a friend, or pull out an appropriate Bible verse
and read it. You know the Bible is precious to me,
Jesus, and I don't mean to belittle it. I just think we
use it as an easy way out instead of getting *involved*
with people and their problems. You gave us the
Bible, but you also gave us eyes with which to see the
tears of others, ears to really listen, and arms to reach
out and comfort.

Let's face it, Jesus. The Christian life just isn't all
that easy. You never said it would be and maybe no
one else did either; but somewhere along the line
many of us got that impression. Christians aren't supposed to be this, that, or the other. But we are. We're
just not honest. I'm not honest. I'm afraid of rejection
by other Christians. I dare say, if the truth were
known, most of them are afraid of the same thing.

Just once I'd like to pick up a good book by a Christian author that started out like this: 'Dear God, I feel
like hell today! I'm angry with my husband, worried
about the future, bitter, resentful, miserable, sick of
my own feelings and failures, and last, but not least,

would like to pack up the kids and dump them on Gesell Institute's doorstep.' Come to think of it, some author *did* say that. You know who it was, don't you? David. He said, 'The sorrows of hell compassed me about . . .' That sounds much nicer than the way I said it, but essentially it means the same thing. History writers threw back the sheets and exposed David's spiritual nudity. I love him because of his weaknesses —not in spite of them. That kind of honesty offers a lot of hope to present-day struggling Christians.

You know, that makes me think of something. This is purely hypothetical. But wouldn't it be interesting if the Scriptures were being written in 1972? I wonder how many Christians would want to have their lives recorded for ever more to be read by countless others through the ages? How surprised some of us would be to discover the sameness between the Old Testament personalities and the 1972 personalities. David had a problem with adultery, yet you said he was a man after your own heart. Moses never felt adequate, yet you used him to lead the children of Israel. Job—well, that poor man was really bewildered when the roof fell in; but you gave him twice as much in the end as in the beginning. Sarah couldn't take you seriously that you could possibly use her. Through her a nation was born. I wonder if those people were as sick of their failures as I am of mine?

Jesus, don't let me be guilty of what I'm complaining about. The next time a friend comes to me, don't let me fall into the easy trap of telling her what *should* be. I hope I will be willing to listen and talk about what *is*.

Do you know what we do down here, Jesus? Of course you do. We shout the glad news, 'Give your life to God and everything will change!' Does it? Yes, certainly, in some respects it does. It makes all the difference in the world. The difference between hope and hopelessness—healthy doubting and despair. It changed for me when my friend, Melissa, told me about you seventeen years ago (bless her!). I discovered the reason for living (I discovered Life) and lost the fear of death. But it didn't take me long after that to develop the mistaken idea that I was supposed to be sinless, loving, joyful, helpful, unselfish, and all those other attributes—all the time. Then the frustration— the doubts, the questions. Then the real growth began —when I started learning to face myself, see my weaknesses, and began to bask in the beauty of honesty before you. I hope someday I will be able to enjoy that same kind of honesty with all other Christians and not fear their rejection and judgment.

Love,

Rosanne

'The God who gave us life, gave us liberty at the same time.'

Jefferson

Freedom I Cannot Live With or Without

Dear Jesus,

I've been rereading Robert Farrar Capon's book *The Third Peacock*. There aren't many books I've come across that I want to read again, but this one says so much I just can't digest it all with one reading.

The book deals with the problem of evil in a world made by 'the original Good Guy' (that's you). It's a good book and I've recommended it to many people who are bewildered with the great question—if God is a good God, and originally made everything so great that He kept saying good, good, good at the end of each act of creation, and if He loves His creation, then why is there so much evil? Why the seeming (or not so seeming) injustices? Why does a twenty-nine-year-old-man die of a heart attack leaving a wife and three small children? Why are people (Christians included) starving to death? Why does a seven-year-old boy die of leukaemia? Where is the peace in this world that you made and said was so good?

You created man, blessed him, told him to be fruitful and multiply and replenish the earth (not over-populate it, mind you), gave him dominion over everything living and moving, looked around at all you had created, sat down, sighed a big sigh of a job well done, and said everything you had made was very good. Now I can go home.

It could appear to us creatures that you quietly slipped away, back to heaven, and here we are in one mess after another. You gave us all this freedom and a will

54

that could say yes or no to you. Why? Surely you knew we wouldn't have sense enough to come in out of the rain on some days.

So from heaven you watched man to see what would happen. Adam and Eve exercised their free will, chose to disobey you, and were told to leave the garden. All hell seemed to break loose in this good world you had made for good man. All that goodness got so bad that eventually you stopped the whole thing and sent a flood and covered it up—with the exception, of course, of Noah *et al.* Then it started all over again. This good world became a circus with a few in the centre ring determined and loyal and loving to the God they acknowledged and remembered as their Creator, a few in the first ring who weren't quite sure how it all stacked up, and a few in the third ring who just rebelled.

Then you picked out Abraham and Sarah and a nation was born through them. And the poor Israelites struggled, wandered, fought, loved, prayed, shook their fists at you, and, I'm sure, wondered why in the world you were taking so long in sending this great deliverer you promised them.

That's it in quite a nutshell. I could try and go into all the theology—but I can't compete with Kierkegaard, so why try? I'll leave the theology to the theologians.

Up to this point it's all very bewildering to me. Then the most important fact of all—you, being a member of the Godhead, who surely had more freedom than any of your creation, chose to leave home and come down here and hang on a cross. Then you rose from the dead and went back home—again.

Actually, from this point on I get even more bewildered than ever. You went back home and sent, in your place, the Holy Spirit to be with us, abide in us, teach us, comfort us, for the remainder of our days on earth. This is exactly what Christians desire (I think)—to be walking in the Spirit. Some desire it a little more than others, perhaps. But I certainly want it, Jesus.

With all my heart I believe the Holy Spirit does abide in me. And I know He never leaves. As I've mentioned in some of my other letters, some days, moments, or hours, the evidence of His presence is quite obvious. Other days I can't do or say one single thing that would give any clue to anyone, let alone myself, that the Holy Spirit lives in me.

BUT. Oh, those wonderful buts! I think I'm learning. Jesus. I don't worry about it as much as I used to. One reason is because I have discovered how terribly honest I can be with you in talking about my growth as a Christian. Also, I realize that most of my Christian life I have struggled to acquire some kind of angelhood. I want to be spiritually perfect. I'm sure the motive is good, but, thank goodness, I've finally realized I may as well quit worrying about not being the great Christian I think I should be. I'll never attain it here on this earth. I work my salvation *out*, yes, and I grow step by step. But I will never come to my full redemption until I receive that new glorious body, like your body, when I get to heaven.

If there is one thing I could thank you for above all else in these past months, it is the fact that I've quit being *tense* about my progress as a Christian. Now ... in my *relaxed* attitude towards myself and with you, don't let me become *lax*.

So, as I said several paragraphs ago, it's all quite bewildering. And surely you realize how bewildered I get sometimes. All I can do is what you have asked me to do—keep coming, keep coming. And I do, even though I can't figure out just exactly why you did it all the way you did and why you chose that particular plan. I don't know and no one else does either.

Why didn't you just create this beautiful world, beautiful creatures, and make us so that we would, by nature, be loving, good, kind, sinless, and without this

56

free will that gets us into so much trouble? Why did you give us free will and then have to come down and die to save us from it? When we get to heaven we will be like you because we will see you as you are. Why didn't you do it that way to begin with? I know—they say you were able to accomplish more in your re-creative act through your death on the cross than you were able to accomplish in your original creation. I just don't know, Jesus. It's such a mystery. You've given me a freedom I can't live with and can't live without.

As you know, Jesus, there are lots of arguments on this question of free will. Some say if you had made us without a free will then we would have loved you because we *had* to—not because we wanted to. But that doesn't hold water for me. If you had not given us a free will in the first place, we wouldn't know what we were missing. Some say, 'Well, there would be no dignity if we were as puppets.' But that doesn't hold water with me either. You, being God, could have figured out a way to make humans in such a way as to cause us to love and respond to you without knowing or feeling that we had to do it. (But then I guess *you* would know we had to and you wouldn't feel especially wanted and loved.)

Please don't misunderstand me, Jesus (and I know you don't). I'm not trying to put myself in the place of the Creator rather than the creature—I'm just turning it over in my mind a bit and finding it all rather stimulating and fascinating to ponder. I'm not very intellectual, you know, but I enjoy reading what others (who are brainy) have written on this subject and at least *trying* to understand. Robert Capon said, 'And what is love if it is not the indulgence of the ultimate risk of giving one's self to another over whom we have no control? (That is why it does no good to explain freedom by saying that God introduced it to make love possible. The statement happens to be true, but it doesn't illuminate much. The question still remains: Why *love*? Why *risk* at all?) The only comfort is that if God is crazy, he is at least no crazier than we are. His deepest and our best are very close.'

I guess that pretty much says it as profoundly as it may be said. It all reminds me of a story I read somewhere—can't remember where. It goes something like this. God was creating one day, having a glorious time, being quite pleased with everything he was doing. Then he got the idea of making a man in his own image. And he made this man a free creature. About that time a flock of angels came rushing down from heaven and said, 'God, what are you doing? You don't dare make this man and give him freedom! Why, he might not love you. He might turn against you. He might try to become a god himself.' They were quite puzzled and upset. Then God turned around, looked at the angels, and said, 'But I'm not through with him yet.'

You're not through with me yet, are you, Jesus? And though I am sometimes confused and deeply thoughtful about it all—I am none the less

Thankfully yours,

Rosanne

P.S. I love you too.

Apples in the summertime
Peaches in the fall
God bless all those handsome men
But you can't love em all!

(often quoted to me by my dad
when I was a little girl)

My Sexuality Baffles Me

Dear Jesus,

There's something I really need to talk to you about. It's a rather sticky subject—at least with me; and I need to know what your mind is in the matter. Can you help me, Jesus?

Gosh, I don't even know where to begin. But I don't have to beat around the bush with you—so let me try and get directly to the point. O.K.?

I like to hug people. Now there's nothing wrong with this—especially when it's my sister, my little boy, a best friend, or my husband's brother, Paul. Usually when I see Paul I give him a big hearty hug and a kiss (not a little peck on the cheek, but a good smack right on the mouth). I love him! Well, this is fine. No one thinks anything of it, it's all in the family, and it's perfectly proper.

You know I'm a demonstrative person. Touching is important to me. When I feel love, deep respect, admiration, gratitude, or any of these things, it's not enough just to sit or stand there and smile at them. I want to express it with the arms you've given me and the mouth that instinctively knew how to pucker from the day I was born. There's nothing wrong with that. You know it and I know it. But you also know it presents a problem. One just can't go around hugging and kissing people—not when those people are of the opposite sex. It's O.K. with brothers-in-law, but what about other men—not related?

For example, L.C. and I went to a fund-raising dinner the other night. The guest speaker was a dear old friend of mine I hadn't seen for years. I was so glad to see him I just wanted to hug him to pieces! I stood there feeling I would burst inside if I couldn't throw my arms around him and give him a squeeze—but I didn't have to—he hugged me! And he gave me a kiss on the cheek. Of course, L.C. was standing right there beside me and he certainly didn't mind. He understood how dearly I loved this man and how happy I was to see him. But I still felt a little uneasy. I guess an old inhibition raised its head and I was afraid someone might be watching and would think I was being too forward. I probably felt this way because of an experience I had when I was about nineteen. It made such a dent I've been afraid ever since to hug a man outside my family.

You remember the experience. I had returned to this town I used to live in and was in the home of friends one evening. Some people dropped by who had been in this fellowship group we had. Among them was this dear boy who was an especially close friend. I loved him! Not 'in love'—just plain loved him in a wholesome, Christian way. I was so glad to see him! Well, when he walked in the door, I threw my arms around him and gave him a big old hug.

Later, this lady came up to me and said, 'You really shouldn't have done that. People will get the wrong idea, and you might cause the boy you hugged to have difficulty with evil thoughts.' Can you imagine, Jesus! Yes, I'm sure you can. So, I decided I'd just have to forego the hugging. Avoid all appearance of evil, you know. And I certainly didn't want to be the cause of having a brother stumble. I was such a young Christian, and anything an older, admired Christian said to me I took as the 'voice of God'. Maybe if I was flat-chested, it wouldn't have made any difference. But you didn't make me that way.

Anyway, it's always been a source of frustration to me. I think we just seem to be 'stuck' on this touching business. I know I used to be extremely naïve. Maybe I still am a little. Somebody told me once there is no such thing as a Platonic relationship between a man and a woman. Is that right, Jesus? If we love someone, feel something 'special' for him—does it always have to have the connotation of sex? It almost makes me angry.

Maybe there *is* a fine line between healthy appreciation and lust. (Heaven help us all to find it!) But as long as I struggle to stay on that fine line—isn't it O.K., Jesus? Sometimes if I slip and fall off, and some thought goes through my mind such as 'Gee, it would be nice to cuddle up with him,' is that bad, Jesus? I know it would be bad to *act* upon the thought—but can we help it if we *think* it sometimes?

See what I mean? This subject gets sticky. You're the only one I can talk to about it without feeling as if I'm walking on eggs. It's frustrating on either side. If I want to express my feelings physically for someone, I feel uncomfortable because I fear other people might think I'm stepping out of line—when my intentions and thoughts are perfectly unadulterated. On the other side, if I do occasionally have one of those thoughts about being in someone else's arms in a romantic situation, I feel guilty because I have the *thought*. Maybe I worry too much about what other people think. Is that it, Jesus? Oh, good heavens— would you please straighten me out!

This friend of mine told me she can hardly stand it when she goes to her Sunday school class any more because the teacher is so good-looking she finds herself fighting with her own thoughts about him making love to her. Surely you don't intend it to be all this complicated—do you, Jesus? Our bodies are the way they are because you made them. If you had intended two people to get married and then completely close their eyes to anyone of the opposite sex from that day forward, then I think at the marriage ceremony you should wave a magic wand. From thenceforth neither partner would ever look twice at or think about anyone else. But it doesn't work that way. My husband still thinks Raquel Welch is an abundantly endowed, gorgeous creature. And my mind can sure get carried away when I think about Charlton Heston squeezing me and whispering sweet nothings in my ear.

Well, dear Jesus, I don't have all the answers to this one. So will you please keep working with me on it and give me understanding? I'll keep looking into your Word, and keep talking to you about it, and eventually I know you'll show me how to live with my sexuality without being so baffled.

Marriage is great. I can hug and kiss and love my husband to pieces all I want ... and it's so good. Thank you for that. It's just that I don't think I should have to feel guilty when I'm attracted to someone else. Surely it isn't wrong to love and appreciate another human being—even if he *does* happen to be of the opposite sex. That seems ridiculous to me. If we kissed everyone on the cheek, as the French do when greeting someone, maybe we wouldn't be so frustrated.

Well, please clue me in, Lord. It's not really that big a concern with me, but I thought it was worth mentioning. And please—don't wait until I'm seventy-eight to let me know what your mind is in this matter. By that time I'm sure I won't have many slow-motion visions of running through a field of daisies with Robert Redford and having him make love to me on the warm, good earth. (I appreciate your sense of humour, Lord.)

Yours,

Rosanne

'... keep ourselves aware of the moment and its small goodnesses.'

Eugenia Price
A Woman's Choice

Thanks for the Enormous Little Things

Dear Jesus,

It just occurred to me this morning that when I'm feeling well, not bogged down with cares of one sort or another, not depressed, not in a stew, and when I have that God's-in-His-heaven-all's-right-with-the-world feeling, I can't think of anything to talk to you about. But just let some crisis flare up and I come running to you full steam ahead. Help! Get me out of this jam!

It's a wonder you don't feel 'used'. But then I'm sure you don't mind too much. It's pretty much the same being a mother, you know. When the kids are outside playing, getting along well with other kids, having a good time, I don't hear too much from them other than an occasional bounding through the front door and a shout of 'I'm hungry!' But just let something go wrong and they come running. 'Mummy, Tommy spit in my eye' or 'Carol kicked me, and girl or no girl I'm gonna sock her right in the face!'

So, right now, Jesus, I'm going to thank you for some of the blessings I take so much for granted when I'm only engrossed in my problems. I'm glad I realized this morning that all too often I only come to you when I'm down and out. This day I feel great—just great! And I want to tell you how much I appreciate you.

First of all, thank you for hot water. It was kind of brisk outside this morning and the house was chilly when I got up. That hot water really felt good.

Thank you for healthy children going off to school,

63

eagerly anticipating their day (even if we were late and I had to drive them, and Clay got into the car barefooted, scrambling to get his shoes and socks on before we got there).

Thank you for dogs, kites, butterflies, and fairy tales. They make the fascinating world of children so much fun, and bring into my adult world a touch of that radiant childlike feeling of adventure and learning.

Thank you for such an abundance of food. We're never hungry without being able to satisfy our hunger. Some days I have griped and grumbled because it seems I spend half my life pushing that crazy grocery trolley around the aisles of the supermarket. But today I want to thank you for being able to push that trolley around and fill it with fresh vegetables, meat, avocados (you know how I *love* avocados), toilet paper, bread, eggs, and hair spray. And in my gratitude I think of those in the world who are hungry. Remember them, Jesus.

Thank you for our garden. I'm looking at it now, Jesus, through the window. Our pretty trees, rose garden, thick grass (except for the bare spots worn with the boys playing football, or 'smear the queer', as they call it). Thank you that they have a garden to play in and don't have to roam the streets.

Thank you for my husband. We had a wonderful weekend together—just here at home, doing things out in the garden and around the house. It was very special. I'm enjoying such a sense of well-being and fulfilment—and knowing I satisfy him as a wife. He's so dear. So patient, intelligent, attentive. I'm so much in love with him, Jesus. Thank you for our marriage.

Thank you for entertainment. We have such a bounty of it in America. Tennis, movies, golf, swimming, parks, football. I really look forward to those football games, Jesus. The excitement of the crowd, cheering, hot dogs, popcorn, the thrill of winning—the disappointment of losing (Green Bay romped our Chiefs 20–0 yesterday). But it's all fun. So much fun! Thank you for fun, Jesus.

Thank you for my washing machine. It sure saves me a lot of time. And thank you for the half-eaten apple, wad of chewing gum wrapper, two pennies, five rocks, one lump of unidentified matter, and a dog-chewed hat off GI Joe I found in the pockets of Elliot's trousers before I threw them in the wash. Gosh! Little people. They're so great! Thank you for that seven-year-old bundle of noise that bursts through the front door after school and yells, 'Mum, I'm home!' Sweeter music my ears have never heard.

Thank you for Sally. She's almost nineteen now a fresher in college, bubbly, full of life, and in love. Thank you for the joy of being able to relive, through her, the early years of growing into adulthood, anticipating marriage, worrying about how I looked and 'if he'll like this dress', and the strengthening struggle of holding back when I was so anxious to jump into bed. Bless her life, Jesus. Thank you for her. Whatever she will encounter throughout the years, may she always know you are there and inviting her to take your hand.

Then there's Clay. Thanks for him. He's seventeen now (going on eighteen). He thinks about girls (in a frightening sort of way), dreams about cars, loves to look at guns in the Sears catalogue, tolerates Sunday school, spends half an hour combing his hair, loves water (in a swimming pool), eats as if there's no tomorrow, and maintains his room so as to justify my one threat of having the health department come and put a quarantine notice on the front door! In short, he's a delight. Guide him with lots of T.L.C. through his adolescence.

Greta's sixteen and dying to be kissed! I'm sure she has been. At least I *hope* so. Boys are cool, parents are inconsistent and rather weird at times, little brothers are a pain in the neck, the mirror is a reflection of all her insecurities, and the telephone was definitely invented to be *used*! Golly, I can remember how unfair it seemed to have to be sixteen. She's such a wonder to behold with her long blonde hair, worn-out jeans, and sometimes puzzled eyes. Take her through these vulnerable years, Jesus, and keep her from giving in to the many temptations that young people have today.

Thank you for blue skies, grey skies, fluffy white clouds, dark rain-filled nights, the cardinal's song, and for time to stop and really look at it all in wonder and amazement.

Thank you for church and the freedom we have to worship there—or anywhere. Thank you for the Bible and being able to have fellowship with others—openly, according to our convictions, without the fear of being punished because of our beliefs.

Yes, Lord—all these 'little things'. Not really little at all, but so readily available I know I sometimes take them for granted. And I'm afraid I sometimes take you for granted too. You're always there—my friend, lover, companion, faithful listener, and comforter. I do want you to be so 'at home' in my life that you know you are welcome to share every part of it.

I was thinking about this the other day while doing some redecorating. I've been painting woodwork, wallpapering, looking at new curtain material, rearranging furniture, etc. And I thought—if my life is truly your 'home' and you *abide* in me, then I should let you be free to 'rearrange' me however you see fit. Perhaps there are some old walls that need tearing down in me, thoughts that need to be thrown out, a coat of new paint on an old resentment, or a fresh, cheery paper on an old, badly stained outlook. Whatever it is, Lord—please *do* be at home in my life. Remind me to be thankful, as I have been today, during those days (and unfortunately I'm sure they will come) when I forget to behold the beauty of the little wonders in life and get all wrapped up in myself instead.

I have to stop now, Jesus. A friend just called and she isn't feeling as on top of it all as I am today. She was crying and has a problem. Thank you for friends. Thank you for being able to share one another's burdens.

Thankfully,

Rosanne

'I am annoyed, Lord, I'm upset—and ashamed of feeling so. Jealousy stings me, a shocked pang that, actually, I rather enjoy. It makes me want to play the martyr, retreating to lick my wounds. And it makes me want to punish him.'

Marjorie Holmes
I've Got to Talk to Somebody, God

Jesus, I Acted like a Jealous Wife

Dear Jesus,

Good morning! It's beautiful today in Kansas City! As much as I hate to admit it, sometimes my moods match the weather. Today the birds are singing, the sun is shining, leaves are shimmering on the trees displaying their autumn dress, the sky is the most brilliant blue I've ever seen, and I feel quite pleased with the whole idea of being a woman.

Yesterday it was so dismal—and still. For hours I didn't hear one sound—not even a bird, or the phone ringing (which is unbelievable). For a while there I thought maybe you'd returned to earth to take your own back to heaven with you and I'd been left behind. All I could see when I looked outside was dormant grass covered with squashy leaves, and everything seemed to be doing nothing other than barely going about the business of being. And I felt the same way— just barely being. I wanted to curl up somewhere in a foetal position, hug a pillow, soak up silence, let my mind drift, and try to fathom such things as why I'm important to you when I'm only one little human out of some three thousand million in the world.

But today is a different story. I didn't even mind it when I 'crunched' across the kitchen floor this morning (on the remains of Halloween popcorn balls). Our dog did a pretty good job of licking it all up—so I'll just let it be for now. Tomorrow is my day to clean house from top to bottom. Today I just want to talk to you. To heck with the dirty laundry—it'll be there tomorrow too.

I do have one little problem I wanted to tell you about. Well, it's not really a problem—not any more. But for a couple of days there I was certainly stewing. My husband and a friend of his took three female business acquaintances out to lunch—and they were gone for three and a half hours! The reason I know is because I kept trying to call him from noon until three-thirty. I had a legitimate reason. Some friends wanted us to have dinner with them that evening, take the kids to a haunted house, and then have cider and doughnuts afterwards. I don't make plans without checking with him first because I'm never sure if he might have to fly out of town—or be tied up in a meeting. So, I kept trying to call—and call—and call.

Well, I don't have to tell you—I was really bugged! He explained the purpose for it, and I have to admit it was reasonable enough. I realize there was nothing wrong with it and it was all perfectly proper—and necessary. It's not as though they'd had a clandestine picnic at the park and played games in the woods.

But being the female I am, I had to struggle for a couple of days with my pettiness and act the role of the jealous wife. I know it was stupid, and I kept telling myself that—over and over. But it didn't seem to do any good. I just kept visualizing them—sitting in some nice restaurant, enjoying good food, laughter, conversation—and well ... I felt left out. Also, I kept thinking—all that time they were having that long, pleasurable lunch, I was at home ironing, running the sweeper, cleaning up the floor after our dog was sick, scouring the bathrooms—and would you believe—polishing my husband's shoes! Then, you know how my mind can really run away with me. All those horribly human thoughts kept trying to find some gooey spot in my brain to cling to. Thoughts such as getting even, turning on my famous silent treatment when he comes home—or putting too much salt on his eggs.

All I could think about was wishing I could find someone (male) to have a nice lunch with who thought I was attractive, intelligent, and stimulating. My list consisted of the postman, the meter reader, the man who repaired the refrigerator last week, the manager at the corner supermarket, my hairdresser—or maybe I could flag down the man who pushes advertising circulars through the front door, and invite him to lunch. But all of that seemed a little absurd—so I gave up! Instead I went out and bought the sexiest nightgown you've ever seen. 'Man, I'll turn him on,' I thought. (Guess I'm getting older, Jesus, and afraid I might lose my desirability.)

Then I came across this verse in the third chapter of James. 'For where jealousy and strife exist, there is disorder and every evil thing. But the wisdom from above is first pure, then peaceable, gentle, reasonable, full of mercy and good fruits, unwavering, without hypocrisy.' Oh, you're wonderful, Jesus! Your words are so relevant in every situation and each feeling. I realized how unreasonable I was being and how ridiculous it was to be jealous. I trust my husband, and we love each other. I'm not worried—he comes home to *me*. And besides, he's certainly entitled to a nice long lunch once in a while, even if it does happen to include a lady. He works such long, hard hours. So I asked you to take all that rubbish out of my mind and replace it with something pure, peaceable, gentle—reasonable. And you did.

Thank you,

Rosanne

'Do not call to mind the former things,
Or ponder things of the past.
Behold, I will do something new,
Now it will spring forth . . .'

Isaiah 43 : 18 and 19
New American Standard Bible

My Past Comes Back to Hurt Me

Dear Jesus,

My dreams kept picking at an old scar last night. When I awakened the hurt was just as great as when the wound was fresh and new. After all these years. It's difficult, when during the day I don't even think about the old things that have passed away and I concentrate on beholding the new things and reaching for them, to have it all come back to hurt me again while I'm asleep. Why did you give us a subconscious?

It was all I could do while preparing breakfast this morning to fight back the tears. I felt as though the experience had just happened last night. The tears were there when I woke up, and I couldn't believe I'd been dreaming. It was so real. 'Weeping may endure for a night, but joy cometh in the morning.' Thank you for nudging me into your Word, thereby not allowing me to wallow in my woe.

You know what I'm talking about—Peter. The boy I was engaged to and waited for—for three years. I suppose that's one of, if not *the*, biggest hurts I've ever had. And I received that letter all over again last night —the part where he said, 'I cannot find God's will or confirmation in marriage for us.' One sentence to end three years of loyalty, loving, and waiting.

Actually, I know I'm lucky if that's the biggest hurt I've ever had. I think of those who have lost hus-

71

bands, wives, children, or suffered the loss of eyes, legs, arms—or mind. It's strange. Consciously, I'm very contented and happy with my husband, family, and life. I wouldn't change them for the world. Most of us, if not all, can look back at the 'what ifs' and 'if onlys' in our lives. But then it's so easy to think the grass might have been greener elsewhere.

When I received that letter I took it to the park, stretched it out page by page, and said, 'O.K., Lord, here it is—my heart is broken and you're the only one who can mend it. And teach me what you would have me to learn from this trial.' Remember, Jesus?

Thank you for your words to me this morning in 1 Peter when I came to you, as then, with my hurt. They were just what I needed.

Blessed be the God and Father of our Lord Jesus Christ, who according to His great mercy has caused us to be born again to a living hope through the resurrection of Jesus Christ from the dead, to obtain an inheritance which is imperishable and undefiled and will not fade away, reserved in heaven for you, who are protected by the power of God through faith for a salvation ready to be revealed in the last time. *In this* you greatly rejoice, even though now for a little while, *if necessary*, you have been distressed by various trials, that the proof of your faith being more precious than gold which is perishable, even though tested by fire, may be found to result in praise and glory and honour at the revelation of Jesus Christ; and though you have not seen Him, you love Him, and though you do not see Him now, but believe in Him, you greatly rejoice with joy inexpressible and full of glory, obtaining as the outcome of your faith the salvation of your souls.

You haven't told us to rejoice in our trials, have you, Jesus? For they do distress us. But we are to rejoice in *you* through whatever trials we have. I could rejoice in you, dear Jesus, in spite of the hurt which distressed me. Rejoice because of my inheritance—not because of my trials. Then the words 'if necessary' stuck out in my mind as I read that. Perhaps it was necessary for me to be given something to hurt a little—even though in a dream—so that I might once again be freshly reminded that I have you, my Saviour and Lord. You have been with me through every hurt and every tear. This morning, in a gripping way, I set my eyes upon what you have waiting for me in heaven.

Peter has been very heavy on my heart all day because of that dream. I've prayed for him, as you know. It makes me wonder. Perhaps he and his wife and family are in great need of prayer right now. Maybe that's why I had the dream. Who knows? I certainly don't, and I'm not going to let my mind get weighed down worrying about it either. If it was for the purpose of praying for them, then thank you for that privilege. Thank you that we can love and help others, though thousands of miles away, by remembering them before your throne of grace. I need to intercede more than I do.

It still hurts—a little. But I'm not going to sit around and think about something that happened so many years ago. This is a new day you have made, Jesus. I will rejoice and be glad. What's on the agenda for today, Lord?

Until next time,

Rosanne

'Bow your neck to His yoke alone, and to no other yoke whatever; and be careful to see that you never bind a yoke on others that is not placed by Jesus Christ.'

Oswald Chambers
My Utmost for His Highest

Some Days I Don't Want Your Yoke

Dear Jesus,

Today I was reading in Matthew. Usually I skip over all that genealogy part—since I can't even pronounce most of the names. But today I decided to try and find out why you wanted it there—if there is something for me to learn. I discovered something. There are four women named in the first fifteen verses of the first chapter of Matthew. Two of them were strangers to the commonwealth of Israel—Rahab was a Canaanitess and a harlot and Ruth was a Moabite. The other two were adulteresses, Tamar and Bathsheba. That's interesting. One would think that your genealogy would consist of great, victorious, virtuous women of God who never fell into such great sins.

David, who is the only one mentioned as a king (I assume because you made the covenant of royalty with him), was married to one of these four women—Bathsheba. What a great example that you accept and use even great sinners, in their repentance, for your human ancestry. That you would even *choose* them and their offspring as part of the lineage whereby you would be born into this world. What an amazing example of your grace!

The truth must surely remain that all you have to work with in this world are sinners. You use us not because we are so usable, but because we're all you

74

have to work with. Most of us who believe in you are heavy-laden with the knowledge of sin in our lives. I guess those who are not—well, maybe they don't spend enough time thinking about whatever it is they should be thinking about. Some Christians are too busy to stop and consider sin in their lives. Others are too busy weeping over their sins. Both are in need of your grace. (I fall into the latter category, you know.) The first because they don't give themselves enough thoughtful time to realize their needs. The latter because they are too busy brow-beating themselves to take hold of your grace and realize your forgiveness and forgetfulness where our sins are concerned.

You know, Jesus, there is this tremendous movement in America today. It's called 'the Jesus movement'. These young people are really *feeling* your new life. It's great. But they're young. So young. One doesn't want to throw cold water on their enthusiasm and tell them it won't last (maybe it will). But I would venture to say that as time goes by, and as they continue on in their Christian experience, they will discover, perhaps much to their dismay, that the Christian life is not always so exciting. Not so hip-hip-hooray and filled with cloud-nine living as they initially experienced. Isn't it important, Jesus, that someone tells these young Christians that the new life in you has very little to do with how we *feel*, but rather how we walk in *faith*? As Charles Spurgeon said, 'Care more for a grain of faith than a ton of excitement.'

It has been my own observation and personal experience that when the newness wears off, one settles down to the daily business of living out your life within us in a world filled with crying, aching, screaming, doubting, hurting, and humdrumness. On the other hand, Jesus, as the years go by and the newness wears off, don't let me lose my first love for you.

You said, 'Come unto me all ye that labour and are heavy laden, take my yoke upon you, learn of me, for I

am meek and lowly of heart, and I will give you rest.'
You didn't say come unto me and I will give you a
great, thrilling, for ever happy experience. Come—
take—learn ... then, and only then, will you give rest.
So often I *come*—and I stop at that. I do not *take* the
yoke. I do not *learn*. Therefore I have no rest.

I have to be honest and admit that some days I can't
get very excited about taking that yoke. I fear it's heavy
—though you said, '... my yoke is easy and my burden
light.' (You know, that bothered me for the longest
time. Then I read something Andrew Young said in
his book *The Poetic Jesus* and it helped me understand a little better. He said of that particular verse
that it is '... a saying not suggesting that it is easy to be
a good Christian, but that his teaching fitted human
nature better, and was less of a burden than the
elaborated Law of the scribes and Pharisees'.) I know
it's the only way—but I want to postpone it as long as
possible. I don't want to bend. I don't want to team up
with the older, wiser ox who knows the way. I don't
want to have to learn—sometimes.

Of course, you know, Jesus, I'm speaking of you as
the other ox. The one who is wiser, knows the way,
and can teach me how to walk in it. It hurts and there
are splinters in that yoke—that is, until it becomes
smooth with time and use.

I guess the truth of the matter is that I would gladly
and freely and even joyfully put your yoke upon me,
come, take and learn, if I could be really sure that it
would guarantee my good feelings. But usually the
taking of your yoke shows me something such as my
bad disposition or my selfishness—and that burr
under my collar gets bigger and bigger until I face up
to my fault and ask you to do something about it.

The truth still seems to remain that you left us to be
free. Free to take the yoke or not to take it. Free to be
stubborn and want to go the other way even when we
are yoked up with you, or free to keep in step. I have

to believe that I am free of your absolute control over my behaviour. I can't believe that you are the eternal Little Jack Horner who goes around sticking his finger in every pie that I, in my bequeathed freedom, manufacture. If that's true, Jesus, if you are that kind of Lord, then part me a few more Red Seas, or light a few more fires with rain-soaked wood, or raise my neighbour's dead husband from the grave.

I know you can still perform miracles, Jesus, but most of the time it seems you have just left us to be the free creatures you wanted us to be, without too much interference. Haven't you just called us to walk by faith in the greatest miracle of all—your death, resurrection, and ascension?

You see, Jesus, what I'm getting at is this. I can well remember the days in my early Christian life when I never doubted, never questioned you, never shook my fist at you. My one and only desire was to live for you, serve you, and go where and whenever you wanted me to. 'Here am I—send me.' That was my attitude. Remember, Jesus? (Perhaps I would do well to remember it and regain some of that newness and fresh zeal.) My eye was on the mission field in India or some such place. Instead I got married to an executive, became a mother and a typical all-American suburban housewife, driving my own car and living in a wall-to-wall carpeted house with three bathrooms. I wanted to set the world on fire and become the great missionary. Frankly (and I've just now realized this), I suppose I'm downright angry at you for not getting me to that mission field, sitting in a little wooden hut, surrounded by needy pagans anxiously awaiting to hear the gospel from my humble mouth. I'm sorry, Jesus. Show me more and more how I can serve you right here. Heaven knows, I don't have to go to India to find needy people. All I have to do is turn around and look at my own children long enough to see their concerns—or walk down the street.

Yes, I can well remember that early enthusiasm, that early anticipation of living my life for you, just as these 'Jesus people' are demonstrating today. I hope they discover something new about your life that they can teach us old-timers. Perhaps they will. I'm a doubting Thomas—but I'm open. But, after all these years of living for you—or of just plain living—if you were to part the Missouri River for me so I could walk through it, I'd probably jump in it and stay there, knowing what I know now about that yoke.

Yet, dear, patient Jesus, the fact still remains I know of no other way than you. So go ahead and keep trying to get that yoke around my neck. Keep trying to break me in so I won't be that stubborn ox trying to throw off the yoke. Keep trying to get the point across to me that I need your experience and I need to be teamed up with you—no matter how difficult.

Thank you for listening to me.

I need you,
Rosanne

'All I have seen teaches me to trust the Creator for all I have not seen.'

Ralph Waldo Emerson

When I Look—Let Me See, Lord

Dear Jesus,

I've a terrible cold and haven't been doing much today other than the essentials. In fact, Elliot and Clay are both home from school with colds too. So the three of us are under the weather at the moment. A while ago I was thinking, 'What a useless day! How unproductive. How lost.' The boys are just lounging around in the family room, and I've been in and out of bed. I've tried to read (but my eyes are watering), tried to sleep (but my nose is too stopped up), tried to think (but I'm too weak to even do much of that).

Then Elliot came in to my room, wanting attention, and feeling pretty miserable. I suggested he bring a game in and we would sit on the bed and play. So he got Clay's *All in the Family* card game, and we sat there and played for a while. There was nothing useless about that time spent with him—nor unproductive. And just that little incident—*seeing* his pleased little face because I was playing with him, and *hearing* his laughter—made me realize something. And that is —how little I really use the senses you've given me. How often I look—without seeing. How often I inhale a fragrance—without smelling it. How often I speak— and say so little. How often I touch—without feeling. How often I hear—but do not listen. And what if all that were taken away—or had never been given me at birth?

What would it be like never really to know the colours of green, red, or yellow? What would it be like never to smell a rose—or bacon frying? Or to hear a child's voice say, 'Mummy,' the sound of thunder, or my husband whispering an endearment in my ear? What would it be like never to touch the velvety softness of freshly mowed grass, stroke our dog's soft coat after he's just had a bath, or really feel the bark on a tree? What would it be like to have never tasted the delicious flavour in foods, the coldness of a snowball, or the toothpaste that makes my mouth feel so clean? How little of what you've given me do I use to its fullest potential—and how often I take it for granted.

I reminisce about the days I lived in Colorado and the Pacific Northwest. And I recall, with nostalgia, the walks along the beach, the majesty of the mountains, the beauty of the forest. And I think about 'the good old days.' I realized today that some time in the future I will probably look back on *these days* as 'the good old days'. Some day when Elliot is a man and brings his children to 'Grandma's house' I will remember today ... when we sat on the bed, both of us with runny, stuffy noses, playing a little game—laughing, chatting, and just enjoying one another. Oh, don't let me just see the mountains, Lord. Let me see each rock! Don't let me just recall the San Juan forest—let me see the trees on my own street!

Yes, I can remember the fire we built and how we sat in awe and amazement as the night gathered around us at our campsite high in the mountains—and I remember the deer coming down from the meadows to drink in the cool stream. But don't let me miss the miracle of several humps of dirt, an imaginative trafficway, and the brilliantly made bridge that Elliot and his little friend created out of mud in a new empty garden patch in our own back garden.

And yes, Lord Jesus, I remember the roaring of the ocean, the waves splashing against gigantic rocks, and picture, in my mind's eye, the vastness of that great body of water. But don't let me pass over the miracle of that mysterious, delightful bowl of 'experiment' that Elliot mixed up with a little leftover Halloween vampire blood, several spoonfuls of vinegar, salt, pepper, and a dash of A-1 sauce, sitting on the kitchen cabinet with a tea bag in it! It may not be the Pacific Ocean—but it has an ocean of little-boy thoughts, intrigue, and ingenuity in it. I don't know what he thinks it's going to *do*—or *become*—but he watches it very carefully from time to time to see if 'something has happened'. The last time he mixed up a batch of his experiments I found it in a glob in the freezer. I guess whatever it was he was hoping it would 'do', he thought it might work better if he froze it!

Thank you for the senses you've given me, Jesus, and thank you for that sixth sense that reminded me today that I too often take for granted the other five.

Recently we've had the pleasure and the privilege of spending quite a bit of time with a new associate of L.C.'s. He's from England and has been in the States on business for a while. I'm just thoroughly fascinated with his English manner, his delightful accent, and some of his word usage—such as 'once a fortnight', 'cheerio', 'what a jolly good time'—or speaking of a 'bit' of this or a 'bit' of that, or how 'keen' something is. Having never been around an Englishman, I was very eager to learn all about his life-style, his wife, his family, their activities. He made a very interesting analogy—I'll never forget it. He said the differences between the English and the Americans are as subtle as our way of speaking. And the more I talked with him, and learned of their life in Europe, the more I realized how much mankind has in common and how really small are the differences—no matter where we live. A smile is the same in any language, or tears, or hunger, or pain. I don't know, Jesus, it just did something to me to have the opportunity to be with someone from another country. It made me realize how little time I take to really see and know another person. How little I really *see* of another's potential as a human being—or how little I'm willing to expose of my own. It has created in me a hunger to know—*really* know—other people, using all the senses you have given me.

I saw a badge in a store the other day—one of those things you can pin on your coat. It said, 'I am a human being. Do not bend, staple, mutilate, or spindle.' Oh, make me more sensitive, Jesus. Give me the hunger you had to really explore the unknown riches behind every human heart—and let me live each day aware of all its possibilities and potentials in my relationships with other people and things.

Speaking of relationships with 'things' makes me think of something amusing. In *The Supper of the Lamb*, Robert Capon gives a glorious description of an onion. He talks about an onion's delicate skin, its two ends, how it is 'a bloom of vectors thrusting upward from base to tip', and how gently and with an open mind you should confront this onion, as though you had never seen one before. It's really delightful! Since reading that book I've never been able to chop, peel, or slice an onion without thinking how Robert Capon would have heart failure if he could see how I attack it. I'm the same with pickles—I mutilate them! And a tomato—L.C. has a fit when I set these uneven, gouged slices of tomato on the table—apparently without any regard for the individual 'things' they are or an appreciation of their creation. Gosh—I hope I don't treat *people* that way. Do I, Lord?

Things, people, places, times . . . oh, let me take hold of it all—grasping all the wonders of life! I don't want to just pass the time, Lord, but rather cherish and possess each living, breathing moment joined together with you in your love for all of its wonder!

Lovingly,
Rosanne

'Let my cry come before Thee, O Lord;
Give me understanding according to Thy word.'

Psalms 119 : 120
New American Standard Bible

My Feelings Don't Make Any Sense

Dear Jesus,

It seems you've been trying to get the same message across to me over and over these past few weeks. As I see other people and talk with them it only confirms what I know deep in my heart: I cannot fulfil, nor can any person fulfil, the God-shaped vacuum inside every living soul. You put that vacuum there and in no way, no way, can it be satisfied apart from the living, loving presence of yourself.

Sometimes I look at people, dear Jesus, and I want, as it were, to reach inside them and touch their very souls—know their deep needs, their yearnings, listen as they pour forth their aches—and then be able to satisfy all their longings. It hurts me inside because I don't have the capacity to do that. And at the same time this is what my own heart cries out for from others. Perhaps this is why I want so to reach out and touch—that in the touching I, too, will be comforted. Forgive me if this is selfish. I don't really want to be selfish. But Jesus, I ask you—are needs selfish? They're so real, so human, so alive in each person. You don't look upon our needs as selfish, do you?

Again, oh again, your promise. '... He is able to supply all your needs according to his riches in glory by Christ Jesus.' Thank you for that promise and the certainty that you will reveal to us, in your own time and way, that you are capable of fulfilling each of our needs—for only you know what they really are.

'Have mercy on me, O Lord, for I am in anguish; my eye, my soul and my body are consumed with grief. For my life wastes away with sorrow and my years with sighing. My strength has failed because of my sin.' You desire truth in the inward parts, Jesus. Show me the truth—the secret sins of my heart I cannot fathom alone. Put within me a new and a right spirit—and a willing one.

O Jesus, when you walked this earth you constantly reached out—touched, felt, healed, made whole, comforted, and met needs. Please make me your instrument to do that for others. Not reaching out and trying to fulfil needs for others or myself in a human way. But you reach out through my hands to touch others—not with human love alone, but with your love, your compassion. If I may give anything to others, let it be by the imparting to them of something of your very self. Let them see you! Let me be used of you in showing others that there are certain inner longings that cannot be fulfilled by anyone or anything other than you.

Thank you for the sweat, tears, agony, grief, and joy from which this letter has been written. And Jesus, dear Jesus, use all of those emotions to give me an enhanced empathy for others.

I saw a lovely human being today—searching, longing, not understanding, being misunderstood. And I hurt for her. 'Tell me what your needs are,' I said. And she could only reply. 'They make no sense!' Of life, of living, she could make no sense. Feelings make no sense at times. We war and become entangled with them. We suppress them and hope they will go away, only to find they come back during those long, quiet hours when we have to be alone with our thoughts—to plague us and make us cry inside. Oh, could I see that lovely human being tomorrow, Lord, let me tell her from a heart beating with joy, grief, laughter, and tears—let me tell her, Jesus Christ is LIFE.

No, Lord. Your way is not easy. But it is not a matter of an *easy* way, but rather of the *only* way ... to heaven.

Love,

Rosanne

'He makes the barren woman abide in the house
as a joyful mother of children. Praise the Lord.'

Psalms 113:9
New American Standard Bible

Peanut Butter Sandwiches and Spilled Milk

Dear Jesus,

I hurt today. Just hurt. No bones or muscles—just a
pang somewhere underneath, where things feel. It's
not my fault you made us so complex—so vulnerable. I
guess it's not your fault either. It's just the way you
and the Father and the Holy Spirit planned things.
Wish I knew why. So ... I alone can bring you my
hurt.

Thank you that you are capable of mending. Mend
me, please. Just when things are going well, just when
I think spiritually everything is pretty well in control
—then bam! It's nothing outward that has happened
—just something that comes over me inside and all of
a sudden I feel as though you're far away and I get
blue and kind of panicky. Thank you that my salvation or my fellowship with you does not depend on
how I *feel*. Thank you that finishing the good work
you started in me is your responsibility—not mine.

I'm sure there is a fine line here. Since you made me
with a free will then it must be up to me to *do* some-
thing where our fellowship is concerned. If I am, as
Paul said, dead to sin and alive unto you, then how
come I keep sinning? What can a dead woman do? O
Jesus, why do you take so long? For seventeen years
I've struggled with this question and read and reread
Romans and other books in the Bible dozens of times,
and books written by other Christians on this subject.
I still don't get it. I know it and understand it in my

86

mind, but I don't know it in my experience.

I realize I'm striving for perfection. I realize I'm striving (and as I understand it, I'm not supposed to strive, but depend on the Spirit). Please bring this home to me. Explain it to me as you would if you were sitting here beside me right now. Make it clear! You didn't promise me confusion, but I'm confused. Help me, for your sake—and for mine too, since I belong to you.

You know the thoughts I've had today that are not right—but horribly human. You know the fear I've had today. You understand how I feel so useless. What have I contributed to mankind—to anyone for that matter? What good am I? Of what use? My life is lived for the most part inside the same walls of the same house with the same dirty floors, dirty clothes, dirty windows, food to be cooked, day after day. The phone never rings with some challenging business decision to be made. No one exciting ever flies in from out of town to sit in a meeting with me. Lunch doesn't find me surrounded with interesting people and stimulating conversation—but rather peanut butter and jelly sandwiches and spilled milk and fussing kids.

Jesus, there it is. See how ungrateful I am? Now—thank you that this is what your gospel is all about. Thank you that now as I bring it all to you I can know your forgiveness, your understanding, and accept your restoration to a more loving, caring, and grateful fellowship with you and those with whom I live. Do you know what L.C. said to me last night when we got into bed? He said, 'This is what it's all about. Having a happy family, happy wife, and someone to be close to at the end of the day.' Isn't that dear, Jesus? Oh, thank you for such an abundance. I could be widowed, childless, and cold and starving to death in some needy foreign country—or America for that matter. It scares me sometimes—the thought of having so much and then being ungrateful for it and dissatisfied.

Actually, I think I just want to be somebody important. Important to whom, I'm not sure. In the eyes of the world or Christendom, I guess. I read a book and think, 'Oh, I could write that!' Or I hear a speech and think, 'Oh, I could have said all that!' How come *they* are there and *I'm* here? Isn't that awful, Jesus? Then I think about something like Proverbs 31. 'Her children rise up and bless her; Her husband also, and he praises her, saying: "Many daughters have done nobly, but you excel them all."' And I think—wow! What could be a greater accomplishment in this world? What greater praise? What greater importance? So, Jesus, thank you that right now, this moment, I can see that clearly. Moment by moment—seeing clearly. Not trying to cut my way through the fog that hasn't even rolled in yet—but seeing YOU clearly, right now.

My heart aches when I read those verses in Proverbs. I wonder what my husband and children would remember most about me? What would my friends? A good epitaph would be, 'Here lies Rosanne: Wife, mother, and would-be many things that she always wanted to be and never could.' O Jesus, don't let me cultivate the desire to BE anything or anyone other than just your woman, basking in your love, and thankful for your fellowship—whenever, wherever—throughout life. I think so much about what Robert Capon said in his book *Bed and Board*: 'We spend a long time wishing we were elsewhere and otherwise.'

I know I have so much to learn—or unlearn—and I can't expect sinless perfection of myself. And save me, please, from a life of legalism. So many Christians get caught up in this terrible thing. It's a struggle you know, between liberty in you, Jesus, and legalism. Where, oh, where is the happy medium?

I have just finished reading Francis Schaeffer's *True Spirituality*. It's really good. He was writing in one part about our list of taboos that we set up for ourselves or others set up for us as Christians. A group of Christians from several countries were discussing this one night. Francis Schaeffer said the more he listened to their conversation and heard their list of no-nos he became aware that all they really wanted was to be able to do these things simply because they were forbidden. He said whether we keep the list or give up the list, it must be for something deeper. The true Christian life is not just keeping or rejecting a list.

That's a good thought, isn't it, Jesus? It's good. But still it leaves us smack in the middle, wiggling somewhere between liberty and legalism. At least I wiggle a lot. BUT (oh, again, thank goodness for the buts) you know all about my wiggling, my struggling, and my searching for the answers. Thank you that I don't need to worry about tomorrow's wiggles. Thank you that today, right now, this moment, I can bring it all to you, and rest assured that you are the KING OF KINGS AND LORD OF LORDS and you are my life! Your blood is sufficient to cleanse, your grace sufficient for needs, your forgiveness sufficient for moment-by-moment guilt. I'm always asking you to do something you've already promised you would do—or have done. So let me just thank you that I am complete in you, and can rest under the comfort of knowing the Father is satisfied with my life because He looks down and sees me in you.

Thank you that I will never come to a point in my Christian life where I can sit back, relax, and pound my chest and praise my perfection. Thank you that the Christian life depends on what you already did on the cross and what the Holy Spirit is *now doing* for me moment by moment. All I ask now is that you keep teaching me and somehow cause my will to become your will. And even when it isn't, I thank you I can tell you about that too, and ask you to make me willing to become willing.

All that liberty and legalism talk is giving me a

headache! Let's go back to something not quite so intellectual ... such as my problem with peanut butter. Thank you for those sandwiches, Jesus, and thank you for *having* children who spill milk. I really wouldn't trade places with anyone. As I'm mopping the mess off the floor, let there be a smile in my heart—*and* on my face, as I remember that the highest calling a woman can have is to be a mother. And make me stop thinking sometimes there are greater things I could be doing.

A happy housewife,

Rosanne

'The mind has a thousand eyes, and the heart but one ...'

F. W. Bourdillon
Light

What I Know and What I Feel Are Two Different Things

Dear Jesus,

When I awakened this morning I thought, as was said in Lamentations, '... it is of the Lord's mercies that we are not consumed, thy compassions fail not, they are new every morning, great is thy faithfulness.' Thank you, Jesus. I know in a very literal way today that were it not for you I would be consumed. Consumed by my own wilfulness, my own sin, my own total inability to reveal your life no matter how hard I try. '... not by might, nor by power, but by my spirit ...' you said. I realize I am not capable of allowing your light to shine through me, daily, any more than I was capable of saving myself—of lifting myself up out of the pit, the miry clay, and setting my feet upon a rock. I realize that, Jesus. But what I *know* in my head and what I *feel* in all the womanly emotions you gave me are two entirely different things so much of the time. Why, Jesus?

Thank you for your Spirit within that will not allow me to let go of my faith in you—no matter how much it seems tossed to and fro at times. You know how hard I try some days to run away from you and give in to my own will—and all too often I do. But then I can't seem to go too far or too long without rushing back to you and hungering for your fellowship.

I've known you for seventeen years now, Jesus. That seems a long time to me. But I suppose to you it's nothing, since you look at everything in the light of eternity—which I can't even comprehend. I look at life in the light of here and now, and I want you to hurry up and conform me to your image because I can hardly bear my own sinfulness. Forgive me for that, my dear Jesus. You already bore my sins upon the cross —and yet I keep trying to bear them now.

It would be nice if you would send me down a bucket of patience from heaven with ribbons around it, and I could all of a sudden become a patient woman. Instead, I know you will send me trials and testings that will produce patience. So, Jesus, I ask you, with all my heart, let that fruit of the Spirit be more evident in my life tomorrow than it has been today. I may cry when you chasten me, and I may run from you. But in the final analysis I am sure, only because of your life in me, I will be able to count it all joy, and thank you for so lovingly teaching me what I needed to learn—or unlearn.

I don't understand, Jesus, why I seem almost obsessed at times with the absurd idea that what I want will actually satisfy me and fulfil my needs more than you can. But I do, Jesus, you know I do. When I have needs so deep, so aching that I'm sure I must be bleeding inside, I rush to other people, other places, other things, knowing those yearnings will find fulfilment. And sometimes they do—for the moment, or the day. Then I'm sickened in my heart—feel empty, and so depressed I want to die—because there is no fulfilment apart from you. How could there be if what Paul said is true—'It is no longer I who lives, but Christ who lives in me'?

Thank you for what I *do* know of your Word, dear Jesus. And you know how I feel about that too. We both know I can't learn everything you have for my discovery in your Word today, tomorrow, or in the next year. What I really want is to be young, yet to have the wisdom and experience of one who has walked with you for seventy years—like my friend Miss Combs. There's no end to my impatience, is there, Lord? Then you know the reason I long for that wisdom and experience is because I'm eager to be more of a living response to you. So, although my impatience is not good—could it be, Lord, that you smile on my motives? I wonder.

You know what I'm going through right now, Jesus —and so much of it is self-inflicted. I know there is victory, and I know you are the answer—but I just haven't learned the meaning of yielding in so many areas of my life. Why don't you teach me, Lord? Why do I continue to struggle when I want to be able to *let*? I just don't know how to let. And I get so confused! Where is the fine line between *letting* your power live through me, and the *self-will* (which must enter in) which you gave me to be exercised? Paul gloried in his infirmities that your power might rest upon. And I say, 'O.K., Lord, I glory in my weaknesses too and fully realize how incapable I am of living for you. But where is the power you promised? I know it's there because you said so and you do not mislead.' But ... it seems such a long time coming.

I'm glad I have the right to come and ask such questions. I used to believe that Christians didn't have the right to question you. But my own children ask me questions—so why can I not come to you, humbly, yet boldly, and ask of you the answers to so much I don't understand about this life in you?

Thank you for today. Thank you for just knowing you're there even though I didn't particularly feel your presence. Thank you for the miracle of faith to believe the unbelievable, the incomprehensible. Thank you for comforting me today when, were it not for you, I would have wept, moaned, and shouted, 'Woe is me!' Thank you for your grace which enabled me to go about my daily tasks of cleaning the house, washing, cooking, wrapping Christmas presents (when

I felt little of the happiness that should go with the season), being polite when the phone rang when in myself I wanted to scream in their ears, and for your comfort and love which kept me from giving in to my desire to lie down and feel sorry for myself—instead of talking to you.

I have to go downstairs and put supper on the table for my family now, Jesus. I'd rather stay here and write more and have this sweet time with you. So thank you again for your grace which will enable me to do it (I trust with a smile) and thank you that I have such a wonderful family to do it for. Help me to listen, *really* listen, to them and to look for their individual needs and concerns and not be all wrapped up in my own.

Until my next letter, Jesus—I love you. Thank you for your faithful friendship.

Still struggling,
Rosanne

'Good-humour makes all things tolerable.'

Henry Ward Beecher

The Upkeep of the Downgrade

Dear Jesus,

You know, a person just hasn't lived until he's been in the hospital for a series of tests! Looking back on it all I can talk about it without the fear and concern I had at the time. I was just sure I had cancer! I wasn't very noble, Jesus, and I'm sure I didn't display any admirable qualities of faith and trust in you. No one could hear those silent utterances of just calling out your name and asking for faith and strength. We spend a lifetime caring for our bodies, you know. We feed them, bathe them, give them rest, exercise, and medicine. When something goes awry with all this equipment you've given us—it's a little disconcerting.

But what an experience! First there's the gynaecologist who leans back in his chair, peers over his glasses, and says, 'I'm not really in a very malignant mood today, but I'm concerned about those tumours on your left ovary.' Then there's the other 'specialist' I was sent to. He was supposed to find out why I was having digestive problems. After having an appendectomy, a tonsillectomy, a gingivectomy, and a cholecystectomy, I was beginning to wonder how many more 'ectomies' were left. First one end and then the other. This time it was the 'other' I was concerned about.

So you go into the hospital and fill out all the papers. They always want to know who your minister is—'Just in case'—and then they strap an I.D. bracelet on your wrist—I assume so they won't lose you or get you mixed up with another 'inmate' and take out the wrong thing. Then you're ushered to your 'suite'. It's not exactly the Hilton (though it costs more)—but it will do. For the next thirty minutes you're bombarded with nurses, attendants, housemen, and lab technicians. They hardly give you enough time to get your clothes off and slip into that gorgeous white negligee that ties down the back (if you're lucky—usually the strings are gone and you just feel the breeze on your backside). Your temperature is taken, your blood pressure, your pulse, and when you have a thermometer stuck in your mouth, a little lady comes in asking what 'valuables' you brought to the hospital with you. Then another lady in white rolls in an I.V. and tells you to make a fist. As she's struggling to find a good vein, you ask, 'What's that for?' 'Your doctor ordered it, Mrs. Jones.' 'But I'm not Mrs. Jones—I'm Mrs. Nelson!' 'Oh—that's right. You're 234B—I want 234A.'

Then someone comes in and tapes a chart on your bathroom door and brings a jug. 'Fill it up, and keep a record of your liquid intake and output,' she says. Ah—then the best part of all. They bring you a dinner menu and you are to fill out what your pleasure is for the evening banquet. By this time you're hungry—and besides you think it might be your last supper (no pun intended, Jesus), so you check off everything on the list. Just as you finish, the head nurse rushes in and tapes a white piece of paper on your headboard that says 'NPO'. 'What's that?' 'That means you're to have nothing by mouth because you're scheduled for tests in the morning.' 'But I just filled out my dinner menu!' 'Sorry, doctor's orders.' 'Can't I even have a cup of hot tea?' 'No, but you may chew on some crushed ice.'

Well, you settle back, read a little, watch TV a little, and hear all about your roommate's inconsiderate husband who went out and got drunk last night. Then they bring you a sleeping pill. 'But I don't want a sleeping pill—I'm already sleepy.' 'Well ... take it anyway, doctor's orders.' So you're off in dreamy sleepy land. That is, until the new nurse from the eleven o'clock shift comes in, shines a flashlight in your eyes, and says, 'Are you asleep, Mrs. Nelson? It's time to take your temperature and pulse.'

The next morning you're wheeled down to X-ray—after they've taken a half pint of blood from your veins and told you you can 'Brush your teeth but don't swallow it.' Well, good grief! I don't make a habit of swallowing my toothpaste! So, you sit in line with twenty other patients, waiting for your X-rays. Finally by 11.30 a.m. your name is called. 'Now, Mrs. Nelson, we want you to drink two glasses of barium.' 'This is my breakfast?' 'It's not really that bad. It even comes in flavours now. Would you prefer vanilla or strawberry?' 'Well, actually, at this point, I'd rather have a tall scotch and water on the rocks.'

And so it goes on. For days they run you through more tests than you knew possible. Finally, on the day before I was to be discharged, the doctor decided he wanted to do a sigmoidoscopy. Do you know what that is, Jesus? Well, you kneel down on this table, they drape white sheets over you, and the doctor takes a long, silver tube with a light on the end of it and ... ugh! It's awful. 'Where are you going to do this?' I ask. 'Oh, I thought we'd do it in the auditorium.' 'Goody—maybe we can sell tickets.'

Well, the time finally arrived and I was sure I would die of embarrassment. To make it a little easier on myself I tried to look on the light side of it and search for a little humour in the whole ordeal. Just before the doctor, two housemen, and two nurses were about to perform the big procedure, I pulled out this little poem I'd written and read it to my 'audience'.

> *He puts you on the table*
> *With your fanny in the air*
> *And everybody takes a look but you—*
> *And that's not fair!*
> *He wants to see my colon—*

I wonder what he'll find,
And I am so embarrassed
I think I'll lose my mind!
He's poked and peeked so much at me
I think I've had my fill—
So if I charge a buck a look
It might pay my doctor bill!

I don't know what all this has to do with living the Christian life, Jesus, but life is such a mystery in many ways—it helps to try and see a little humour in all that mystery.

Besides, I didn't have much else to write to you about today. Everything is great with my family and me. But I'd better get busy and face those dirty dishes and put an onion in the oven so my husband will think supper is cooking when he gets home. If I tell him I've just been sitting in my room all day, writing 'a letter to Jesus', he might think I've flipped and I'll end up back in the hospital!

So, that's all for now, Jesus. I just wanted to keep in touch. Besides, I'm sure you enjoy hearing from me once in a while when I'm in a cheery frame of mind instead of telling you how gloomy everything is. Sometimes it does get pretty rough—but not always. I'd probably get bored if life rolled along so smooth all the time.

The mountains and the valleys, the floods and the drought—all a part of life. Show me how to live through its heights and depths . . .

Always thinking of you,

Rosanne

'Men would be angels; angels would be gods.'

Pope

I'm so Discontented

Dear Jesus,

I'm discontented with my own discontentment.

Wherever the company wants to move us I know I should be satisfied and happy because I'm a Christian —but I'm really having a struggle with this, Jesus. I just don't want to move! When we came to Kansas City and bought this house, I vowed then my next move would be to heaven. I'm so tired of feeling like a nomad. I'm so tired of being a puppet on a string under the mighty hands of the big corporation. A man no sooner becomes efficient in his new job than they transfer him somewhere else because his expertise is needed there. What they end up with, it seems, is a company of inefficient experts. I just don't want to live anywhere other than right here on good old West 97th Terrace.

The bedrooms need painting, and I can't get the least bit excited about it because I don't know how much longer we'll be living here. I had such exciting plans for redoing the boys' bedrooms. Now I just walk in there and say 'Yuuk!' I wanted to put some bulbs out this autumn, but we probably won't be here in the spring to see them grow and bloom. We may as well buy a trailer and hitch it on the back of the car and live in camp grounds. That way we would always be mobile. Oh, that reminds me of that old saying about Christians—keep your heart open and your bags packed. Baloney! Darn! Darn! Darn!

Well, I got that off my chest. Jesus, do you know what I've been thinking about the past week? Paul said, 'I have learned in whatever state I am therewith to be content.' Surely he didn't mean Tennessee too, did he? That's where they're talking about sending us. I'm kidding. I realize when he said 'state' he was referring to circumstances. Anyway, I've been thinking about that verse a lot. This is what I want—contentment.

If you could speak to us as you did to Abram and tell us exactly where you want us to go and for what reason, then I'd gladly go. I think. Then I wonder if I could be as blindly obedient as he was when you told him to '... get out of thy country, and from thy relatives, and from thy father's house, unto a land that I will show you'. And then it says, 'So Abram departed.' He must have had a contented heart too or he couldn't have gone without asking at least one or two questions. I wonder if he thought he would be able to snuggle down and live contentedly and peacefully for the rest of his life after he reached Canaan? I wonder if he realized that I would be reading about him all these years later and be encouraged by the example he set?

His *peace* was not in a *place* or he might never have left Haran. I know, Jesus, I'm not going to find contentment in a place either. I want the contentment Paul was talking about and that Abram knew. Paul knew times of affluence and times of need, but whatever his circumstances, he was content. He claimed he actually *learned* to be content. Golly. I wish I could say that. Then he went on to say, 'I can do all things through Him who strengthens me.' That's the key. His contentment was a result of you, Jesus. If he learned it, can't I learn it too? Teach me. I want to be so involved with just knowing you, loving you, and living for you, that no matter where I am or whatever my circumstances, I will be content.

Sometimes I wonder if part of my discontentment isn't a result of having too much. Americans are so thing-minded. Someone is always dreaming up a new gadget. We suffer from what Joseph Bayly called 'the poverty of affluence'. He said, 'You know, one problem that is left in the United States is that we have so very much, including so very much in the Scripture. Mary in her Magnificat said, "He has filled the hungry with good things, but the rich He sent empty away."'

Yes, sometimes, Jesus, I am terribly discontented. I'm sorry about that. I don't want to be that way. Thank you for understanding this human feeling and for imparting a little more of yourself to me as I've been writing this letter. So right now, I can honestly thank you for the mystery of what's around the corner. I don't know where we will be living, and right now I don't care. It's not a matter of where I am—but *who* I'm with. And I'm always with you and you're always with me. Help me to remember that as I'm knee-deep in packing cases and grumbling profanities under my breath. I'll need reminding.

I need you,

Rosanne

'He has made everything beautiful in its time.
He has also set eternity in their heart ...'

Ecclesiastes 3 : 11
New American Standard Bible

It's Winter Outside, but Spring in My Heart

Dear Jesus,

You've made a magnificent world for us, and this morning it all turned a dazzling white here in our little segment. I was so excited when I looked out of the window and saw the birds scratching the snow off the feeder—hungrily pecking for their breakfast of sunflower seeds. I couldn't wait to go in and awaken Elliot for school. But he was so groggy. He pushed his head under the pillow and said, 'Oh, I'm too sleepy. I don't want to get up.' (He called me into his room at 3.30 a.m. because Cricket [our dog] was taking all his covers. So neither of us had as much sleep as we usually do.) But I encouraged him to get up and look out of the window. So he hopped out of bed, and I was anxious to see the expression on his face at the sight of our first snow.

I can well remember how thrilling that was as a child. And it still is. It's as though you pour down a blanket of blessing during the night for a surprise when we wake up. I think you must enjoy surprising us, Jesus, just as we do *our* children. Maybe it will stick, and the boys can build a snowman when they get home from school. You should have seen Cricket when I let him outside this morning. He turned around and looked at me as if to say, 'What's this stuff?! You expect me to do it out here in the cold?' (We do talk to each other, you know.)

Tomorrow night we're having a church banquet

and I've a lot of work to do today in preparation. And, as usual, I have errands, cleaning, and washing. But I'm really excited about my day. I want to have some logs burning in the fireplace when the boys get home from school and hot chocolate with marshmallows on top for their after-school snack. Maybe (if I have time) I'll bake cookies to go along with it. They love to walk in the front door after school and smell something yummy coming from the kitchen.

This will be a good night for potato soup. I think I'll fix it for supper—L.C. just loves it! Do you eat in heaven, Jesus? I've often wondered. I certainly hope so. I can't imagine an eternity without food! If that parable you told about the great banquet, recorded in Luke 14, is a literal analogy, then it truly will be a feast. Is it literal, Jesus, or were you symbolically speaking of a spiritual supper? Well, whichever it is, I accept your invitation. I'll be there, and am looking forward to it! (I've always thought how nice it will be to get to heaven and no longer have digestive problems. Then I can eat all the pig's knuckles and sauerkraut I want. I don't get it often since I'm the only one in my family who likes it—but then, we all have our little idiosyncrasies.)

L.C.'s been working so hard lately, Jesus. He always does—but it's been terribly heavy the past few weeks. I do worry about him. He doesn't get enough sleep. As soon as the present crisis is over (and before the next one arises), he wants to go away for a long weekend. In fact, he insisted I get my passport so we can take off for some exotic island. (It's fun to dream.) Seeing all this snow makes me want to go skiing—but L.C. doesn't ski. Actually, I'd settle for the motel three miles down the street where we could just spend a long weekend eating, sleeping, reading, and loving. (We've always thought it would be fun to check in somewhere as 'Mr. Jones and Miss Smith'—just to add a little sparkle. Isn't that naughty, Jesus?) But you understand, and I can't help but think you might be looking on with a little twinkle in your eye. There's something intriguing about a no-no. That's just human nature, and you know, of course, our human nature and our Christian nature walk all over each other sometimes.

Well, if I'm going to get my work done and find time to bake those cookies, I must get busy. Besides, I'm anxious to bundle up in my boots, wool scarf, and mittens, see my breath in the crisp air, and sing that song about walking in a winter wonderland.

And O Jesus, you not only gave us a lovely snow this morning, but seeing it reminded me of that beautiful passage in Isaiah 55:

> For as the rain and the snow come down from heaven, and do not return there without watering the earth, and making it bear and sprout, and furnishing seed to the sower and bread to the eater; so shall My word be which goes forth from My mouth; it shall not return to Me empty, without accomplishing what I desire, and without succeeding in the matter for which I sent it. For you will go out with joy, and be led forth with peace; the mountains and the hills will break forth into shouts of joy before you, and all the trees of the field will clap their hands; instead of the thornbush the cypress will come up; and instead of the nettle the myrtle will come up; and it will be a memorial to the Lord, for an everlasting sign which will not be cut off.

How beautiful, Lord! The snow comes down from heaven and stays to enrich the earth—just as your words come to me in all of their splendour, comfort, instruction, and hope. And they stay with me to nurture me and produce spiritual growth. Thank you, Jesus. Today I will need go forth with you in joy and peace with a song in my heart.

As always,

Rosanne

'... so often I am afraid to take real risks without the sense of Your presence. I guess I am praying for faith, Lord, so that I can act on the reality of Your love ... even when I cannot see it with my senses.'

Keith Miller
Habitation of Dragons

I'm Numb and Depressed

Dear Jesus,

I feel numb today—depressed. I'm reminded of your Word which says, 'And the Lord direct your hearts into the love of God, and into the patient waiting for Christ.' Do that for me now, please. Direct my heart right into your love. Surely there, in your warmth, I won't be numb. But if the numbness doesn't go away, or the depression, as quickly as I would like it to, then help me to wait patiently.

Some days, Jesus, as I wrestle with these feelings, and am so all alone with them, I feel like the original voice in the wilderness—crying out—'Somebody, please, *somebody*, bring back the joy!' I don't know if I can explain it, Jesus. But I'll try. Always I have the joy of being redeemed and the joy and assurance of heaven. Always I have the joy of knowing you love me deeply and *care*. But at the same time I can feel so dry. 'A joyful heart is good medicine, but a broken spirit dries up the bones.' Don't let my spirit be broken, Jesus. My selfish pride, my own wilfulness, yes. But not my spirit. Your spirit bears witness with my spirit that I am a child of God. And don't let me be overcome by my times of numbness and depression. Let me learn in it and grow in it—and grow out of it—back into the good medicine of a joyful heart.

Thank you for being unchanging, because I change so much from day to day. I realize if I had to trust and depend upon my feelings, life would indeed be unbearable—at least for me, because you know how emotional I am. I wish I weren't—sometimes. Other times I would have to admit I enjoy my mood swings. Anyway, that's the way I am, and I thank you for that too, knowing your promise to '. . . perfect what concerns me'.

Jesus, why must I be so weak in certain areas? Why can't I know in experience that when I am weak in myself then the power of Christ rests upon me? Paul had his thorn in the flesh. I don't know what it was. (Maybe his thorn wasn't due to his own human weakness.) But you knew. And you know what my thorn in the flesh is—my weakness. I guess we all have our thorns. Show me the way to get it out, Jesus. I've prayed that you will remove it—and you haven't. I've claimed that verse that says, '. . . it is God who works in you both to *will* and to *do* of His good pleasure.' That hasn't worked. I've thought then that it must just be a matter of sheer will power, so I have mustered up all I am humanly capable of—that doesn't work either. I have claimed the power of the Holy Spirit to do it in me—that hasn't worked. I feel like Job—I go backward, forward, and every other way and I can't find you or your answer in this problem. But Job did say, didn't he, '. . . but He knows the way I take and when He has tried me I shall come forth as gold.' Right now that's my only comfort, my only hope.

If I am seeing no liberation from my own self-destructive ways because I don't really, deep inside, want liberty—then all I can do is talk to you about that too. I don't know what else to pray. 'O that I might have my request; and that God would grant me the thing that I long for.' O Jesus, you know my heart. I don't—not really. So you look into it and bring to your light what I need to see about my heart that is

106

thwarting the fulfilment of your promises in this problem. I know the promises and I know you stand behind every one you give with the enabling power of the Spirit. So I know it's not because you are inadequate. O Lord, it's just me. I know other Christians who struggle with weaknesses and battle with habits they don't want to have. Oh, I feel for certain friends just now as I'm writing this. Friends with great problems. Thank you for reminding me to '...look not every man on his own things, but every man also on the things of others'. Thank you for your life in me which enables me to feel more for my friend right now than I feel for myself.

'I would seek unto God, and unto God would I commit my cause: Which doeth great things and unsearchable: marvellous things without number: Who giveth rain upon the earth, and sendeth waters upon the field.'

I look out of my window just now, Jesus, and see the trees stripped of their green robe and watch the birds fluttering about. I wonder why you made it thus for them? Why do they have to fly south in the winter? It would be better if they could stay here all year round and didn't have to make that change. But they don't resist the change, do they? They just go. They trust the wings you have given them. Show me how to trust the wings you have given me—to '...mount up with wings of eagles'. And oh, today, today, dear Jesus, show me how to run and not be weary. Today I would rather mount up and fly away—just fly away. Fly from my numbness and depression. Today I will know the truth of Ecclesiastes 7:3: 'Better is sorrow than laughter; for by the facial sadness the heart is made glad.'

I know you didn't come into the world, dear Jesus, to promise us nothing but sorrow and tears. But you did tell us we would have a cross to bear. I know, from past experience, some days it is better to know sorrow.

For afterwards, ah yes, afterwards, I will have learned something deeply engraved in a weeping heart. Then —the peaceable fruit of righteousness will be yielded.

Teach me to trust,

Rosanne

'How many cares does a mother's heart know?
      Nobody knows but Mother.
How many joys from her mother love flow?
      Nobody knows but Mother.
How many prayers for each little white bed?
How many tears for her babes has she shed?
How many kisses for each curly head?
      Nobody knows but Mother.'

Mary Morrison
from her poem *Nobody Knows but Mother*

'Enjoy life with the woman whom you love all the
days of your fleeting life which He has given to you
under the sun; for this is your reward in life, and
in your toil in which you have laboured under
the sun.'

Ecclesiastes 9 : 9
New American Standard Bible

A Queenly Wife and Mother

Dear Jesus,
    I kept Elliot home from school today because he has
a stuffy nose and sore throat. He's downstairs now
making a little man out of a pencil, two empty spools
of thread, six clothespegs, and a straw. I just sat there
watching him, Jesus, really *seeing* his sweet childlike
imagination and creativity and marvelling at the glorious little guy he is. Too often I'm afraid I look at him
and what he's doing and don't really *see* because I'm
busy doing something else or preoccupied. I noticed he
had drawn a face on one of the clothespegs, and it was
smiling. Elliot's faces always smile. I hope that's a good
sign. I hope he grows up with a good feeling about
himself, his parents, his life—and most of all about
you.

A little while ago he brought me a picture he had drawn of you. At the top of the page he had written, 'Love is good God.' You are standing—looking down on the earth. You have long hair, big eyes, three teeth (I wonder if he did that because he is missing his front teeth?), and arms that reach your knees. You have a wide belt on, flare-leg trousers, shoes with big laces, your hands are huge, your head bigger than the rest of your body, and you have a pointed nose. But none the less you look pleasant.

Then he drew a picture of heaven. The sun is smiling and you are standing on top of a cloud with Charlie (a pet rabbit that died) and Missy (our dog that died), and your hands are reaching out petting them. How precious are those pictures!—I'd rather have them than an original Rembrandt.

I have such a quietness in my heart today, Lord. I'm so deeply satisfied with my role in life of being a wife and mother. You know, I've never really wanted to do anything else. Sure, it's a lot of work, but '...the dream comes through much effort' as Solomon said. And I never tell anyone I'm 'just a housewife'. Saying 'just' makes it sound as though I'm not proud of it and feel insignificant. And I don't feel that way. It's a vital role—and I know *you* think it's important. You're the one who thought up the whole idea of husbands, wives, children, and homes.

It seems to be inherent in a man to be the 'head'—to be aggressive. And I know it's inherent in me to want *my* man that way—taking the lead. I wouldn't want to be a man for anything! I enjoy being a woman! Oh, I know, I may disagree with him and give him a hard time on certain decisions. But in the final analysis I find a lot of comfort and a sense of obedience to you when I respect and acknowledge him as the head of our home. Needless to say, I'm certainly no picture of the ideal wife (whatever that is), never baulking on issues. In fact, Jesus, you check me many times on this.

And you always remind me how you intend the relationship to be. Of course, I realize I'm lucky. L.C. fulfils his part too. He doesn't lord it over me and treat me as though you took that bone out of the bottom of Adam's foot instead of his rib! He's very considerate towards me ... most of the time.

I've never had a lot of confidence in myself as a mother, Jesus. Perhaps I read too many books on parenthood and children. Sometimes all those different viewpoints confuse me. So I just keep coming back to your book and trusting you for all that wisdom I need—hoping my love for my family will cover the multitude of mistakes I've made. You know, Jesus, there are three things I've asked you for where the children are concerned. First: that they would grow up loving you and accepting your love. Second: that they would grow up knowing we love them—in spite of our mistakes. Third: that they would grow up loving themselves and having a sense of well-being. If they have all that (which is a lot), they'll make it in life.

Remember, in the delivery room, when the doctor put Elliot in my arms and I counted all his little toes and fingers, saw all that thick, black hair, and gently snuggled him to my breast? I asked you at that moment that he grow up to be your man. I have such dreams and hopes for him, Lord. As I've watched him grow, I've tried to keep from pushing him into my mould and have asked you to mould him, Jesus, through my hands. I hope I haven't made too many mistakes. At least no mistakes that will be impossible to undo. But how wrong to fear that. Nothing is impossible with you—is it?

I've often thought how disappointed I will be if he doesn't go on to college. But that wouldn't be fair either, would it, Jesus? Whether he becomes a very capable ditchdigger or a renowned church leader, my real prayer is that he will just be *yours*—wholly and with deep conviction. I think it must be more difficult for children today than when I was small. Today there is so much emphasis on education and so much pressure to be successful (whatever that is). Elliot is only in second grade and he's already learning this new maths that I can't even understand. Golly, when I was in second grade I don't think we did much more than work on the alphabet, add two and two, and bounce balls. I hope he will always find in you, dear Jesus, a loving and comforting retreat (within his own mind) from all that pressure, and still press towards the mark for the prize of the high calling of his Christian life.

Being a wife and mother is so rewarding, Jesus. There's so much joy to be found in a dozen little things every day. Be it preparing a dish of cranberry sauce for L.C. (knowing how he dearly loves it) and seeing the pleased expression on his face when he comes home for supper, or going into Elliot's room at night, turning on the lights, and looking in the closet and under the bed to reassure him there are no monsters—there is a lot of happiness in a multitude of little things. Little—but endless in their effect.

You know that song, Jesus, 'The Best Things in Life Are Free'? I've always liked it—and how true it is. It's all the expressions of love and of life you give to us and we give to each other that cannot be replaced by all the riches of this world. For example, last night L.C. and I attended a dinner party at a convention in Kansas City. I wore a new long evening dress my mother had made for me as a Christmas present, and L.C. really liked it. He remarked several times during the evening how pretty I looked and how much he admired the dress. This morning he got up quite early to attend a breakfast meeting. He didn't want to awaken me (wasn't that thoughtful?), so I didn't even get to see him before he left. When I got up I found a little note on the dresser. It said, 'Rosie dear—I love you. I was very proud of you last night. L.C.' Isn't that sweet? What material riches in this life could possibly take the place of that one little note, scribbled on the back of a bill? I wouldn't trade it for all the books of love poems in the entire world! Not even Lord Byron's own personal first edition of *Don Juan*. I have so much, Jesus—so very much. I'm the wealthiest woman in the world! A mere thank you falls so short of what I feel in the depth of my being.

You know, Jesus, I went through a period of time (and I told you about it) when I felt a pang of dissatisfaction in my marriage. But it all worked together for good. Now, looking back on it, I can hardly believe I ever had those thoughts. It seems unreal. I feel such a close sense of oneness with L.C. And as he so aptly told me the other night, 'I wish I could crawl inside your skin and be you.' I know how he felt. And there really aren't words to describe it. It's just a deep desire to be so completely one that you wish you could somehow share the other's skin. Does that make sense, Jesus? I'm sure you understand. It's beautiful. Thank you for thinking up the idea of marriage. It may have its problems—but with us, for every problem there have been a hundred joys. It just seems I'm more verbal about difficulties. That's a mistake, I know. If I could learn to be equally verbal about my joys and the goodnesses, the problems would seem insignificant.

When I think about the vastness of everything that has gone on before me in place and time, and all that will go on after me—I *could* feel insignificant in my role of wife and mother. But I don't—because I know you see me going about my tasks, and you think it's all very important. You see me washing the little fingerprints off the walls, cleaning my husband's bathroom cabinet for him, standing at the kitchen sink, sorting out laundry, picking up his suit at the cleaners, grocery shopping, taking the boys in for haircuts, sitting up with a sick child, polishing my nails, and changing into something fresh and feminine before L.C. gets home from work. One could look upon these tasks as trivial, I suppose. But to me they're not. All these little things go to make up the bigness of life itself. And I know you see me doing it all with just as much care and love for me in my role as housewife as you have for Queen Elizabeth sitting upon her throne. This is my throne! The children are the lords of my court and my husband my king! And today I do indeed feel like a queen.

I'm so contented,

Rosanne

'It doesn't seem fair for some people to have nice homes with safety, Lord, while other people can't get out of a slum like this except in a coffin.'

Malcolm Boyd
Are You Running with Me, Jesus?

What Can I Do About the Slums, Jesus?

Dear Jesus,

It's late, the kids are asleep, my husband is on a business trip, and I'm up to my neck in heavy thoughts. I'd like to talk to you about it if these jumbled-up thoughts running through my mind can find their way into words, and if the words don't get stuck in my throat. It's precious to have a time of silence to think out loud—but when I start thinking deeply it can get pretty disturbing.

If I could only cry—a good, long soul cry. Maybe I'd feel better. Maybe I'd feel a sense of accomplishing something for the people I'm thinking about tonight —even if I only cried for them. At least I would have done something! What people? Those people out there—across the city, *my* city. You know, Jesus. That man, that woman, the little girl and her two older brothers. The ones sitting there in that broken-down dump they call home. Where they sweat in the summer and freeze in the winter. That family of five human beings sharing one room. The wife's washing out the dirty underwear so they can wear it again tomorrow. The man's boozing it up in front of the TV (thank God, at least he's got *that* to help him keep his sanity). The boys go out in the street to kick the can— or you know what else. The little girl sucks her thumb and cries and ... and what? What does a little girl do without dolls, doll houses, miniature sewing machines, bicycles, and fluffy stuffed animals?

What about them, Jesus? What do they have to do with me? What do I have to do with them? Jesus! What *can* I do? Shall I pack up some of Elliot's old toys and take them over? Shall I take them a week's supply of groceries? What would I say to them? Shall I give them my pity in exchange for their pride? Or do they have any pride left, Jesus? Shall I tell them God loves them, as I sit there in my stylish dress and the woman self-consciously tries to straighten her hair and fingers her worn-out housecoat? Would they just think me some kind of nut who drove across town to bring them a few material love offerings and share the Good News? It isn't that I would care what they would think of me. It's just—well, I would care how they *feel*.

And then what would I do after I'd done all that? Go back to my nice house in the suburbs, walk through my front door on to my carpets, turn on the automatic dishwasher, take a few steaks out of the freezer to throw on the grill for supper, pour a cup of coffee, sit back in my easy chair, and feel perhaps I'd done something today for those less fortunate than me?

I'm not trying to sound flippant, Jesus, I'm just trying, period. Trying to make sense out of it. 'To whomsoever much is given, much will be required.' What do you require of me, Jesus? Is it enough that I care—really care? Would that be enough for them? Would it make them feel any better or make it possible for them to quit drowning in their debris? Would it help for them to know that there is one affluent person in this world who genuinely gives a damn? You know about them, Jesus, and millions like them in the world. You care more than I do. Is there some way you can make them feel valuable? Is there some way they can believe you love them and care—even when they worry about food on the table and clothes for the children? Is there some way to get food on the table and clothes on their backs? Shall I take these things to

116

them—and take your love with me, and tell them I wish there was some way we could exchange lives? I've had my affluence, you've had your poverty—now it's time to turn the tables.

They're starving, physically and psychologically and they're scared. I'm scared because I'm not starving —because I've got so much (which doesn't seem fair), and yet I talk about discontentment, hurting, frustrations, and doubts. God! I don't know what suffering is. Help them. Help me. Remember them. Help them to remember you. The only way they can get out of those slums is to die—and be carried out. Somehow, show them, Jesus, that although they may not be able to get out of the slums, they can be rid of the torment of their minds in being there and in feeling hopeless. Give them hope, Jesus. And if you want to give them more than hope, if you want to give them new underwear, warm blankets, meat, and potatoes, then show me how to take them these things without my pity dripping out of the basket along with them. Not pity. Somehow, somehow, Jesus, let your *love* so shine out of me that they will see my good works AND GLORIFY YOU.

I'm going to bed now, Jesus. I wish I could cry myself to sleep. Paul wept over the needy and the lost. When was the last time I shed actual tears over someone's need and salvation? Let it be tonight, Lord. Tonight let me know something of your heart and the kind of heart Paul had that he could weep over the lost. Let me cry myself to sleep with a heart filled with your compassion. Melt my heart.

Please, Jesus,

Rosanne

'The day will give place to the night and the night again to the day. Is it summer? It will be winter. Is it winter? Stay a while, and it will be summer. Every purpose has its time.'

Matthew Henry

Happiness Is...

Dear Jesus,

Someone asked me the other day, 'What makes you happy?' I could have answered quickly by saying, 'I'm happy when things are going well with my husband's work, when I'm looking forward to an exciting vacation, when I've just recarpeted the house, or when we're spending a casual, relaxing evening with good friends.' Happiness takes many forms, and my state of mind is frequently affected by 'happenings'. But actually, Lord, if I was dependent upon *events* as my source of happiness, I know there wouldn't be much deep-down satisfaction, but rather a surface, temporary 'state of mind'.

So I'm certain happiness must have a lot to do with hope. You can't have one without the other, can you? Happiness isn't just a 'what' but a 'Who'. It isn't a 'some*thing*' but a 'Some*one*'—you, Jesus. That isn't to say that because I know you and love you I'm never sad. But underneath the sadness brought about by circumstances, there is always a basic happiness because my *hope* is rooted in you.

I think I'm changing, Lord. Maybe I'm growing. It used to be that when some positive episode came my way, producing a happy state of mind, I became scared. I wanted to hold the eventuality very carefully in my hand, protecting it—like a vulnerable bubble that might burst if you turned too quickly one way or

118

the other. Maybe I always did that out of guilt, Lord. Maybe because, for so long, I had these feelings of unworthiness and being undeserving, I just couldn't learn how to accept and enjoy the goodnesses. I think you finally made me stop doing that, Jesus. Whether the spoke on the 'wheel of nature', as James said, is up or down, I'm learning to go through life with a little more steadiness.

I actually used to feel closer to you when there was some huge weight upon my shoulders—or depression. It was as though I could find you more easily when I was hurting than when I was happy. But lately, I've been quite elated. Some affirmative events have taken place in my life, and I feel nearer to you than ever. So I think I'm beginning, just a little bit perhaps, to see things from your point of view and realize that you are there, rejoicing with me in the happiness as well as comforting me in any sadness.

Just lately, Lord, I have received some special recognition. Nothing world-shaking (except to me), but some really good things have been taking place in my life. I was sharing the news with my friend Grace, and she said, 'Rosanne, I hope you will be able to enjoy this.' Well, she knows me pretty well. And I thought about that statement she made. I asked myself if I was going to allow myself to jump in and enjoy it—or was I going to turn on that old recording that said, 'be humble, be humble', which actually, by my twisted interpretation, has always meant you should walk around with your head bowed, your eyes on the ground, and feel unworthy. But not this time, Lord! This time I'm going to make these blessings an altar where I can praise you for all this abundant life—this manna you've poured upon me. And if there is any attention drawn to me, I hope people will see *you* there when they look at me. I don't say that as a lot of 'pretentious religious poppycock'. You know I always hope something of your nature will work its way

119

through me.

So I think now I will answer my friend who asked the question 'What makes you happy?' by saying, 'Happiness is ... being established in a lasting friendship with Jesus Christ,' or 'Happiness is ... not being disappointed'. And when I say that, I think of that verse in Romans 5, '. . . hope does not disappoint.' I can never remember a time when you've disappointed me, Lord. I've disappointed myself, others have disappointed me, circumstances have taken an unpleasant turn. But when I hold tightly on to you in spite of myself, others, and events, I have that constant *hope*, which is the foundation for happiness. And what is hope? Paul said it is '. . . Christ in you'.

I can remember as a child how a sudden, empty feeling came over me when I was riding the merry-go-round at a carnival and the music stopped and the horses gradually ceased going up and down. I could hardly enjoy the ride for the apprehension of its coming to an end. And I'm afraid I did carry much of that childish attitude into my adult life, Lord. But I've learned a lot. Right now all lights are 'go' and everything looks rosy. But I know, eventually, things will sort of settle down, the newness of events will wear off, and perhaps even be replaced by a few trials. But I won't cry when the ride is over this time. Now I think you've taught me enough that I can be grateful for the fun of it and enjoy it without the fear of its coming to an end.

Matthew Henry wrote about this so beautifully. He said, 'We live in a world of changes. The several events of time, and the conditions of human life, are vastly different from one another, and we are continually passing and repassing between them. In the wheel of nature sometimes one spoke is uppermost and by and by the contrary; there is a constant ebbing and flowing, waxing and waning from one extreme to the other. When we are in prosperity we should be easy, and yet not secure—not to be secure because we live in a world of changes, and yet to be easy … in a humble dependence upon God, neither lifted up with hopes, nor cast down with fears, but with evenness of mind.'

I lived my life for so long as though I was on probation and you were my parole officer. If I was a good girl, happy things would happen. If I was a bad girl, sad things would happen. But it just didn't quite seem to work out that way. Sometimes it seemed when I thought I was being bad, not praying enough, not reading the Bible enough, not witnessing enough, not being sweet enough, lo and behold, the blessings would come! Or when I thought I was being good, doing all the 'right' things, and feeling quite confident that I was living the shining, Christ-filled life, instead of having all my 'burdens roll away', I'll be darned if they didn't roll right on top of me! So thank you, Jesus, for not putting me on probation and going around with a thick file on me keeping account of my goodness and my badness. If the blessings you pour out depended upon my moral excellence, uprightness, or the lack of them, I'm afraid my bucket would be empty. You just keep giving and giving and giving, with an unconditional love, while I keep trying and trying and trying—to see more of you.

So, life is constant change—except for you. Some of these changes are your doing—some by my own will. And as Solomon said (and I love that passage):

There is an appointed time for everything. And there is a time for every event under heaven—

A time to give birth, and a time to die;
A time to plant, and a time to uproot what is planted.
A time to kill, and a time to heal;
A time to tear down, and a time to build up.
A time to weep, and a time to laugh;
A time to mourn, and a time to dance.

A time to throw stones, and a time to gather stones;
A time to embrace, and a time to shun embracing.
A time to search, and a time to give up as lost;
A time to keep, and a time to throw away.
A time to tear apart, and a time to sew together;
A time to be silent, and a time to speak.
A time to love, and a time to hate;
A time for war, and a time for peace.

This seems to be my 'time to laugh', Lord. And I am happy. Not just because of certain events that have taken place in my life lately (although they have their influence), but basically because I am rooted in my love for and belief in you. And when this 'time to laugh' changes into a 'time to weep', you will still be there—my hope and my happiness.

Love,
Rosanne

'... singing with thankfulness in your hearts to God.'

Colossians 3 : 16
New American Standard Bible

I Just Want to Praise You, Jesus

Dear Jesus,

May I just praise you this day? May I not talk about my problems but just look at your face? I just want to thank you for yourself, for what you saved me from, for what you are saving me *to*, and for my ultimate salvation in the heavenly homeland.

I praise you, Jesus Christ. I praise you!

When I can make no sense out of circumstances, thank you for the sense I can make out of just you. When I doubt myself and others and find pieces of the puzzle of life missing, thank you that I need never doubt *you* nor try to comprehend what you have asked me, in faith, to trust you for and believe. I know you'll give those pieces when I'm ready for them.

Thank you for all the little things and all the big things—for whatever is involved in your plan and purpose, which as a human I cannot comprehend. Thank you that all I need do is *look*. Look at the moon, the sun, the stars, the way buds bloom in spring, the way thunder proclaims your majesty, the way rain falls and snow flies, trees shed their leaves, mothers create new life, the way wind blows and tides change, the way mud is formed—and roses bloom. Yes, I just look, and I can believe. There is a Someone far greater, so supernatural, who put it all into place and being. I simply believe that because you are you, I am me.

I praise you, Jesus Christ! From your manger to the magnificence of '... being lifted up on high and given the name that surpasses every name, so that at the name of JESUS every knee should bow, of those in heaven, of those on earth, and of those under the earth, and that every tongue should confess that JESUS CHRIST IS LORD to the glory of God the Father'.

I praise you, Jesus Christ!

'Looking unto Jesus, the author and finisher of our faith; who for the joy that was set before him endured the cross, despising the shame, and is set down at the right hand of the throne of God.'

I praise you, Jesus Christ!

'For in him dwelleth all the fullness of the Godhead bodily. And ye are complete in him, which is the head of all principality and power.'

I praise you, Jesus Christ!

'In my Father's house are many mansions: if it were not so, I would have told you. I go to prepare a place for you. And if I go and prepare a place for you, I will come again, and receive you unto myself; that where I am, there ye may be also.'

I praise you, Jesus Christ.

'By His doing you are in Christ Jesus, who became to us wisdom from God, and righteousness and sanctification, and redemption.'

I praise you, Jesus Christ!

'In whom we have redemption through his blood, the forgiveness of sins, according to the riches of his grace.'

I praise you, Jesus Christ!

I praise you and I thank you for being with me through my life. Your ear has never tired of my questions. Your heart has never grown weary with my confusion.

For this reason, I bow my knees before the Father from whom every family in heaven and on earth derives its name, that He would grant you, according to the riches of His glory, to be strengthened with power through faith; and that you, being rooted and grounded in love, may be able to comprehend with all saints what is the breadth and length and height and depth, and to know the love of Christ which surpasses knowledge, that you may be filled up to all the fullness of God. Now to Him who is able to do exceeding abundantly beyond all that we ask or think, according to the power that works within us, to Him be the glory in the church and in Christ Jesus to all generations for ever and ever. Amen.

Yes, Jesus Christ. You are the Almighty I AM ... and I am yours!

All my love, for all time,

Rosanne